Advance Prais

I'm Trying to Lead . . . Is Anybody Following?

A clear, creative and compelling case for "transformational leadership," impressively grounded in a wide range of contemporary leadership studies, Christian spirituality, and the Gospels. Thoughtful questions at the end of each chapter make the book an ideal resource for group study not only by church leaders but by congregations.

—**E. Glenn Hinson**
Emeritus Professor of
Spirituality and Church History
Baptist Theological Seminary at Richmond

I began reading Chuck Bugg's new book with some skepticism that there could be any new material on the subject of leadership. And yet, I finished feeling encouraged by his fresh and effective vision for leadership to grow in community with others as we face change together.

—**Rev. Deborah Gaddis Reeves**, M. Div.
Board Certified Chaplain
Association of Professional Chaplains

Dr. Chuck Bugg invites readers on a journey into the deeper challenges of transformational leadership with congregations. Drawing from his experiences—leading everything from a student body to a large congregation—his clear, warm, confessional style and personal stories enrich the solid and diverse theories of postmodern leadership. With humility he honestly faces his limits and challenges. With confidence he offers bold alternatives to traditional management approaches.

This volume tackles tough, divisive issues like poverty, sexuality, and the environment. His daring questions, such as "Was Jesus a transformational leader?" summons readers to build their own theological foundation for leading.

—**G. Wade Rowatt**, Ph.D.
Senior Professor of Pastoral Care and Counseling
Baptist Seminary of Kentucky

Smyth & Helwys Publishing, Inc.
6316 Peake Road
Macon, Georgia 31210-3960
1-800-747-3016

Library of Congress Cataloging-in-Publication Data

Bugg, Charles B.
I'm trying to lead . . . is anybody following? :
the challenge of congregational leadership / by Charles B. Bugg.
pages cm
ISBN 978-1-57312-731-8 (pbk. : alk. paper)
1. Christian leadership. I. Title.
BV652.1.B837 2014
253--dc23

2014016466

Charles B. Bugg

I'm **Trying** to Lead . . .

IS ANYBODY FOLLOWING?

The Challenge of
Congregational Leadership in
the Postmodern World

Other books by *Charles B. Bugg*

Preaching & Intimacy: Preparing the Message and the Messenger, 1999

Witness of a Fragile Servant: A Personal Look at Pastoral Preaching, 2003

Lingering Grief: Listening for God in the Pain, 2007

Transformational Leadership: Leading with Integrity, 2010

Dedication

To my children, Laura Beth and David, who have taught me leadership in their own ways.

Laura Beth graduated from Harvard Divinity School. She met Bryan Gaensler, a native of Australia, and they now live in Sydney with our grandson, Finn. My only regret is that I didn't have a vote in where they chose to live. If you want to stick with A's (as in Australia), I would have picked Atlanta, Austin, or some other place on this side of the world.

Laura Beth's streak of independence is seen in her retaining her maiden name. Greater love hath no daughter than to stay a "Bugg."

Laura Beth is a Senior Lecturer in the Sociology Department at the University of Sydney. Her specialty is "Sociology of Religion." She's an articulate advocate for the oppressed and marginalized, and she challenges her dad with her caring way of supporting those who often get left on the sidelines of life.

Her husband Bryan is an astrophysicist. He started his own center, travels the world, and meets with astrophysicists and astronomers to talk about things that people like him talk about. I'm very proud of his entrepreneurial spirit, but I'm especially grateful for his being such a wonderful husband and father.

Because of a brain tumor that my son David had at age ten, he has not been able to verbalize his ideas as well as Laura Beth. Yet David is a profile in courage. He is sensitive, caring, and always looking for ways to help Diane and me. David lives with us, and we are so grateful not only that we have him but also for the way he reminds us to face the adversities of life.

Acknowledgments

I talk about congregational leadership in a time of change. The change that is true on a "macro" level is also true in the stories of our lives. In August 2013, my only sibling, my brother Bob, passed from this life into everlasting life where he now waits for me and all of his friends and family.

In December 2009, Bob was diagnosed with a rare, usually fatal disease. In 2010, he and his wife, Patra, spent over a month at the Mayo Clinic in Minnesota. The doctors shut down his kidneys, and he was put on dialysis. When Patra and Bob returned home to Clearwater, Florida, they were surrounded by the love of their three children, six grandchildren, a host of loving friends, and the church where they were members.

Bob fought the good fight, but he lost the battle nearly three years later. My brother was eight years younger than I. When I flew to Florida to visit him in the intensive care unit, I told him before I left, "You have made a difference in people's lives. I love you, and I'll see you at the 'glad reunion.'"

Bob was an attorney, and since I was a minister, we were both very verbal. Sometimes we disagreed about matters of faith or social issues. I doubt that he would endorse everything in this book. But after each of us had our say, we would go back to talking about baseball or events in the past. The one thing we never did was to doubt each other's commitment to our faith in the God of Jesus Christ.

Needless to say, I deeply miss picking up the phone and talking with my brother. I miss his loving and warm way with people. He was my brother; I loved him and always admired the authentic way that he lived out his faith.

Change comes, and Bob died. I'm writing about change in the twenty-first-century church, and suddenly, I'm reminded just how difficult and tough change can be.

In writing this book, I thought not only about Bob but also about the countless clergy and laypeople who pour their lives into trying to make their churches more of the body of Christ. Some of them get little affirmation. We read about the church leaders who abuse children or are caught with pornography. I'd like to see an article about the Reverend Bob or the Reverend Betty who spent the week visiting hospitals, conducting a funeral, preaching a sermon, and then went home to get ready to start a week much like the one before.

Churches are changing, but my faith is in the Christ of the church and the folks who serve so faithfully. My life and my family's life were changed at the West Flagler Park Baptist Church in Miami, Florida. Whatever else you pick up in this book, I hope you will sense my commitment to churches like West Flagler Park, where the Spirit of God moved and people's lives were never the same again.

On a personal level, I continue to be grateful for my wife, Diane. In my twenties, I'm sure I was more concerned about how attractive a potential wife was on the outside rather than on the inside. However, I hit the jackpot, or, to put it in more spiritual terms, I married someone who embodies the spirit of the Christ and who loves and encourages me to be the best I can be.

I'm also grateful to Maria Lockridge, who took my scratchy writing and put it into a form that we could submit to the publisher. Maria has been so kind to take my increasingly bad handwriting and try to make sense of it.

For all who read this book, I'm grateful. Talking about the issues of leadership means we will have differences of opinion. I want to remember, however, that this side of eternity, none of us has a corner on truth. If we lose our care for each other, we have lost the great treasure.

Contents

Foreword

by Bo Prosser

Chuck Bugg is my hero! Through the years, I have known him as my pastor, as a ministerial colleague, as my preaching coach, as a faculty colleague, as a leader, as a follower, and as a friend. In every setting, he has always been gracious to me with his time and his insights. We have sat through more church meetings than either of us want to admit. We've shared many times of fellowship, we've shared our families, and we've shared our hearts. He is a treasured friend and mentor. Each time I am with him, I go away feeling more inspired and confident. He is everything a hero should be.

The pages that follow are a gift from my hero and friend to those of us seeking to become more effective leaders. Chuck practices good leadership even as he is sharing about leadership in an engaging and encouraging way. As he unpacks leadership in the congregation, he does so with typical humility. While he presents many bold ideas of leadership, he cites others who have helped form his approach. He also gives readers time to pause and reflect using the questions at the end of each chapter.

Chuck writes with clarity as he tackles some of the difficult concepts of leadership and helps readers understand the work of writers like Ronald Heifetz (adaptive leadership), Daniel Goleman (emotional intelligence), and Richard Rohr and Henri Nouwen (spirituality and devotion). Chuck communicates these concepts in ways that are practical, understandable, and applicable to the leadership context.

He also writes with courage as he responds to some of the most challenging issues facing the church today. He is not afraid to speak plainly about human sexuality, the disparity of wealth and poverty, the environment, violence, and the dilemmas of postmodernity. He is confessional about his own journey and invitational to the reader to join him in that journey. His research and responses indicate that navigating these challenges takes a lifetime. Clearly, Chuck is still in process on these issues and calls each of us to reflection and introspection as well. While he offers his personal convictions, he asks each of us to think for ourselves.

This book is also highly congregational. Chuck's love for the church is evident in each page. He calls us to "see the Christ in the other person" and to invest ourselves in the "transforming hope that Christ brings us." He challenges us to "become transformational leaders" while living out the compelling concepts of "servant leadership." He charges us to summon up our inner "Commander, Coach, Counselor, and Conductor" in order to clarify vision and serve in transformational ministries. Leadership is an art that can't be grasped quickly or in "seven easy steps."

Finally, and above all, this book is about Jesus Christ. Chuck leaves the reader with the compelling question, "Was Jesus a transformational leader?" He shares his thoughts about Jesus' leadership style using the qualities that have emerged during the course of the book. With the support of Scriptures and scholars, Chuck makes the leadership model of Christ accessible to us. At the end of this writing, we will all be convinced that we can lead like Jesus, "guiding people to transform their lives into something bigger, better, and more meaningful in the kingdom of God."

With scholarship and spiritual depth, with clarity and courage, with story and inspiration, Chuck Bugg moves us from where we are to where we need to be. He urges us into the reality of our congregational contexts with confidence that we can lead and make a difference. His confidence in the church is palpable and motivates me to want to be a better leader, minister, husband, and friend. After finishing this book, I feel his confidence in me. That's what heroes do: they instill in us a belief that, while all may not be right in the world, we can make a difference.

Introduction

I came early in life to the issue of leadership. I came late in life to the issue of leadership. This sounds contradictory. Let me explain. At the age of fifteen, I committed my life to what our church called "full-time Christian service." That meant you were going to be a minister. In that day, the primary options were pastor or missionary.

My home church talked often about being "called to ministry." Since I never heard a voice from beyond or saw handwriting on the wall, I interpreted my call largely through my adolescent intuition or through the affirmation of my gifts by others. "You're a good speaker," people said, and that became the blessing.

Soon after my call, I started preaching at my home church, the Rescue Mission in Miami, the county jail, and any other place that was willing to take a chance on a young minister filled with enthusiasm but virtually devoid of insight. As I moved through college, I became a part of the youth-revival movement and took way too seriously the kind people who said I would be the next Billy Graham.

When I attended seminary, I was exposed to critical methodology and learned that doing an exegesis on a Bible passage was more complicated that I had imagined. I also became drawn to classes in Pastoral Care, took a unit of Clinical Pastoral Education, and found that human beings, including myself, were more complex that I had thought.

Along the way, I took the required class in Church Administration. The person who taught it was a retired pastor who seemed to be a kind and good man. However, there was no particular emphasis on how to be an effective leader in the church. We never spent time assessing our strengths or areas of growth, and, frankly, I felt deprived.

While a student in seminary, I was pastor of a small church that wanted me to be their preacher and pastoral care giver. We never articulated a vision for growth since the community was isolated and the members were mostly related to each other. What I did was "manage" the church along with lay leaders, making sure that worship services were structured and teachers were recruited for Sunday school classes, and doing the kinds of things that made sure we were operating week to week.

Finally, I finished my work on two degrees at seminary, and in the middle of the summer of 1972, my "great with child" spouse, our two-and-a-half-year-old daughter, and I moved to the east coast of Central Florida, where I began as pastor of my first full-time church. Suddenly, I was in a world where I was trying to lead a church that had experienced contentious and difficult times. I had a semblance of a staff, most of them volunteers, five deacons, numerous committees, and a church that had split over theological and personal differences.

In the midst of trying to get my family settled in a rental house replete with all kinds of tropical varmints and oppressive heat, I went to work trying to lead the church. Fortunately, most of the people were caring and loving. Because I had a "nice wife" and "cute children" (the church's terms, although I agreed), the congregation cut me a lot of slack. I'm sure I made more than my share of mistakes, but the congregation came together, we grew in numbers, and we were eventually able to hire some excellent part-time staff ministers.

Here's what I knew about leadership. Because I had served as president of my university and seminary student bodies, I knew enough about parliamentary procedure to preside at meetings. On most days, I was a non-anxious presence who evaded answering questions from some fiery-eyed fundamentalist who wanted to know if the rapture preceded the tribulation. Early in my ministry, Diane commented to me after a business meeting, "You can talk more without saying anything." I believe that Diane was saying, "When you talk, nobody really understands which side you're on, and everybody believes you agree with them." Not exactly a resounding "Profile in Courage," but this approach got me through the tall weeds.

You will recognize my general approach to leadership. Talking to the church, I'd say something like, "We need a plan." I'd suggest a five-year plan or, in my more optimistic moments, a ten-year plan. (Frankly, I never did a ten-year plan, since my longest tenure at a church was seven years.)

So, with congregational input, the leadership and I would work on a five-year plan. I recognized the need for ownership, so I wanted to involve as many people as possible in the visioning process. We'd identify certain goals, develop strategies to attempt to achieve those goals, develop time lines, assign certain people or groups in the church primary responsibility for meeting objectives, and then chart some measures for determining whether we had achieved success.

Honestly, I spent more of my time as pastor managing issues rather than leading the church to bring in the Reign of God. Malfunctioning air conditioners, somebody who didn't think his Sunday school teacher really believed the Bible, and countless other things—like people's giving to the budget—kept me from always seeing the big picture. It became clear to me why Major League Baseball refers to guys like Dusty Baker or Bobby Cox as the "managers" of their teams. I didn't want to be an ecclesiastical manager. I wanted to win the World Series, but I was spending a lot of time keeping the dugout together and in shape.

Regarding leadership and my five-year plans, I did all I knew to do. While better than nothing, I failed to take into account all the wonderful things we now know about boundaries, self-differentiation, systems' theory, and adaptive leadership. I had one mold into which to pour my leadership Jell-O and no idea how to make possible the collaboration of management and leadership.

Fifty years later, I hope I think differently and more deeply about leadership. It's not that I've abandoned planning. Planning is essential, but I've come to see how much more complex the whole process of planning is. The Christian landscape has changed. Bright, energetic people are graduating from seminaries and divinity schools, and some are bringing their good gifts to the frontline of a church.

But most of the churches are not like their mothers' churches or the ones that I first served as pastor. Call it "post-Christian culture" or whatever descriptive phrase you want to use, but churches are generally more marginalized than they were fifty years ago, and many people are less interested in institutionalized religious expressions than before.

A recent study reported by the Pew Forum on Religion and Public Life underscores this seismic shift in church affiliation. Cathy Lynn Grossman wrote, "For decades, if not centuries, American's top religious brand has been 'Protestant.' No more."[1] Since 2007, people in the United States who identify themselves as "Protestants" have declined from 53 percent to 48 percent. Perhaps more disturbing is that Americans who claim no religious affiliation have increased in the same time frame from 15.3 percent of adults to 20 percent. Pew Forum senior researcher points out that one in three (32%) of those who claim no religious affiliation are under the age of thirty. In the researcher's opinion, this group is not likely to "age into any religious affiliation."[2]

Add to that the attraction of "mega-churches." Extremely large churches appeal to people who like numerous programmatic offerings and worship services that are staffed with a charismatic preacher and a worship team that provide a variety of delivery systems with a high level of performance.[3] The "bandwagon" idea of psychology is alive and well. Go to almost any town or city, and folks will point you to one or two congregations that are the "it" places of worship.

While some of us as clergy may not find this type of congregation appealing to our liturgical, theological, or ecclesiastical tastes, it does raise the issue of how we choose to lead or not lead. We may eschew the model of a tight-knit group of elders and ministers who make all the important decisions, but the fact is that it's not enough simply to know what we oppose.

And that's the main purpose of the book. I want to try to offer a view of leadership that has theological integrity, recognizes and honors the members of the congregation, and reinforces the brave hearts of ministers who offer visions, take risks, and understand that those of us who follow Christ have chosen a leader who also experienced success and failure.

I wish I could offer you a book that covers the "Seven Steps to Successful Church Leadership." I would probably sell more books that way, and you would also like the promise of the title. The problem is that bookstores are filled with leadership books that may offer a few good suggestions but can't guarantee unmitigated success. Leadership is a treacherous journey, and only the bravest people book passage for the trip.

Notes

1. Cathy Lynn Grossman, "As Protestants Decline, Those with No Religion Gain," *USA Today*, 9 October 2012, A-1, http://www.usatoday.com/story/news/nation/2012/10/08/nones-protestant-religion-pew/1618445/ (accessed 27 March 2014).

2. Ibid

3. A University of Washington Study posited, "Worship services at megachurches can trigger feelings of transcendence and changes in brain chemistry—a spiritual 'high' that keeps congregants coming back for more" (*Christian Century*, 19 September 2012, p. 18).

Chapter 1

A Spiritual Foundation for Leadership

In his provocative book, *Let Your Life Speak*, Parker Palmer writes about his own struggle, "I wanted deeper congruence between my inner and outer life."[1] This search for congruence is imperative for effective leadership. While leaders are often perceived in terms of their influence on others, the breeding ground for effective leadership is the peace that comes when we are "at home" with ourselves.

What we do as leaders is then a reflection of who we are as people—what Parker Palmer calls the deeper congruence between our inner and outer lives.

I was reminded of the pain of incongruity one summer when I was a student at seminary. As part of a special study I was doing on the children of alcoholics, I attended a meeting where most of the children were younger than twelve years old. I sat in the back of the room to observe.

At 7:00 p.m., a well-dressed boy stood up and called the meeting to order. With clockwork proficiency and the poise of someone well beyond his years, he ran the meeting, recognized people to speak, and moved through the agenda. Needless to say, I was impressed. I've been in meetings where adult moderators didn't know the first thing about Robert's Rules of Order, and most of the time was spent arguing about process rather than substance.

Not at this meeting run by children. It was the highlight reel of efficiency and order. The agenda was followed; the children at the meeting spoke succinctly and stayed on message; the young moderator controlled the time allocated to each item; and, wonder of wonders, the entire meeting finished in one hour.

Afterward, I drove home impressed by the tightness of the meeting. Then I became afraid. I had not witnessed children free to play and enjoy for at least a time the loose ends of life. I had observed grown-up control freaks in the bodies of children who had been forced too quickly to bring order into the chaos of their lives.

I had also seen myself. Growing up in a home with an alcoholic father, I had responded by creating a strict sense of order and control in some of the confusion around me. Nobody had to tell me to do my homework. No one had to admonish me to work hard and to achieve. In a frightening sense, the carefree ways of a child became the control of a little adult for whom order and achievement were priorities.

Obviously, the span of time since my childhood has given me some opportunity to evaluate and, hopefully, to change some of the ways that I grew up viewing life. But we never completely discard the characteristics that have been embedded in us, and we live with some of the fears and uncertainties that have become a part of the fabric of our being.

That brings me back to Palmer's perceptive observation about congruity between our inner and outer lives. For me, this is the primal struggle of our spiritual foundation and leadership. The secret, which is not much of a secret at all, is to identify and allow God to begin to change the inner parts of us that inhibit or even sabotage our ability to lead. The struggle of this change is often the labor of a lifetime because one of the most difficult challenges is to let go of entrenched, even destructive patterns.

Take, for example, the child of an alcoholic parent. That child may respond to the family's confusion in a variety of ways. Suppose that child reacts to the external chaos by trying to control as much of her life as possible. Taken to the extreme, this child functions with a strong sense of rule and order. When something unexpected breaks that order, the child feels out of control and threatened by the chaos. Instead of chaos being a momentary condition that everybody has to endure at some time or another, it becomes a fundamental threat to the child's stability and certainty. In other words, it can't be tolerated because it throws her universe completely off axis.

Remembering Our Inadequacy

Walk into any group of people and ask the leaders to raise their hands, and you will encounter reluctance. One reason for that is people's desire to appear humble. After all, who wants to stick his hand up as if to say, "I'll take charge while the rest of you follow"?

A second reason that we are reluctant to say that we have leadership capacities is the perverted way in which some so-called leaders have abused the trust that people have placed in them. If leadership is getting people to follow, the history of the world is replete with individuals like Adolf Hitler, James Jones, and many others whose charisma and twisted minds created untold pain. Only a psychopathic personality would be drawn to this demented form of leadership.

In fact, this destructive type of "leadership" may not be leadership at all. A leader has to have the best interests of the people in mind and be grounded by a moral, compassionate compass. The leader's task is to make life better and to expose values that enrich and empower people to live in a way that makes them more caring and ultimately better contributors to society. People like Hitler and Jones certainly possessed charisma, but their work produced tragic and devastating results.

The third and, I believe, possibly the greatest hindrance to people's exercising leadership is our illusion that leaders seldom if ever fail. Many of us view a leader as someone who orchestrates any situation perfectly and rarely makes misjudgments or mistakes. When we perceive that our leaders are perfect, how does that affect our self-image?

We know ourselves. We see our inadequacies. Like Moses on the back side of Midian, we want to argue with God or whoever is asking us to assume a position of leadership, saying that we believe that we aren't talented or gifted enough for the task. We fear that we may fail, and some of us have learned to fear failure more than almost anything. What if we began to look at ourselves as human beings, filled with potential but also filled with inadequacies? What if we tried something and didn't succeed at the level we expected? Or what if we attempted to make some differences in a group or situation, and we were criticized because people didn't agree with us? Does that make us failures?

The fact is that it's hard to measure success. Regardless of what we do, few ventures are absolute, 100% successes. We critique ourselves appropriately at times, and then we try to learn from our failures. Also, some people will criticize the leaders in congregations regardless of what the leaders do. Remember that jealousy, envy, and second-guessing are alive and well among folks who never have responsibility for a job but still think they know how to do it better than anyone else.

The desire to do things well and please people in the process is commendable. The opposite is not to care how we do things or to have any regard for those whom we offend. A leader is not called to trade competency and care for an attitude that ignores the realities of a task and the relationships with the people he or she leads.

Some of us, however, are seduced by the need for perfection and the desire for everyone to approve of us. This need freezes us and makes us afraid of any attempt at leadership. No one can guarantee success. Failure is always a possibility, but we have to work to separate our personal identities from our performances. Failing doesn't make us failures any more than success makes us perfect. Again, we all have both limitations and potential, and a leader is the person who is willing to take the risks in order to succeed, fail, or fall somewhere between the extremes of success and failure, as most often happens.

Learning to lead like this requires understanding that we function on a foundation of transcendence. In other words, do we believe that leadership is simply the exercise of our skill set and training, or does God play a significant part in giving us the courage to risk something big for something good? Do we feel embraced by God so that, whether we succeed or fail humanly speaking, we know that we are unconditionally loved by the Greatest Lover?

This is vitally important to the enterprise of risk-taking, which is at the core of leadership. We all deal with the issue of self-esteem. The image of a self is shaped by nature, by our primary caregivers, and by the way we adjust our images through prayer, introspection, guidance from others, and the multiple ways in which we receive feedback from people who love us and whom we trust.

So are leaders born rather than made? Do people by their nature possess the qualities that can be developed into those of an effective leader? On the other hand, can we do anything to develop leadership ability in someone who seems to lack the intrinsic qualities that we associate with a "take-charge" leader? For those who want to read more on this intriguing subject, Sharon Daloz Parks has written a fascinating book, *Leadership Can Be Taught.*[2] Her hypothesis is that almost anyone can be taught many of the skills of effective leadership, regardless of the person's nature or early nurture.

Definition of Leadership

Daloz Parks's contention that leadership can be taught raises an issue that we will explore throughout this book. Leadership comes in different ways and is exerted through various gifts. When I taught at several seminaries and divinity schools, my primary area was homiletics or preaching. Students would come to class possessing various constellations of gifts. Some of them were bright and poised, and, while nervous, they were still eager to stand in front of a group to preach.

Other students told me that this was the one course in the entire curriculum that they dreaded the most. The notion of having to prepare a sermon and then deliver it in front of their peers caused them nightmares. I noticed several interesting things in this experience of teaching. First, some of the best preachers were those who felt awkward and afraid. They worked hard at having something important to say, and there were times when a sermon was preached, and the class had to take a few minutes to reflect on the power of what we had heard. Conversely, some of the student preachers who were most eager to let their light shine left us with a display of style but little substance. After teaching and preaching for many years, I finally concluded that there is no such thing as the "best" preacher.

While intrinsic gifts are a factor in leadership, they are not the only components. Obviously, strong, articulate, visionary leaders function better in large groups where clarity and charisma are essential elements. In small gatherings where important decisions are frequently generated, however, the quiet, steady voices may be the ones that help disparate groups focus on what is essential by lowering their voices so that real dialogue and conversation can take place.

Both the charismatic, visionary person who draws the attention of the crowd and the quieter individual who helps group members focus and talk to each other rather than at each other are examples of leadership. The first leader may be the one who most often occupies a formal position, but the second person is often the leader as he or she generates camaraderie among competing voices and allows people the space to brainstorm creative solutions for different issues.

Spiritual Qualities of a Leader

The Sacred Heart: A Leader's Character

I am forever indebted to Dr. Ronald Heifetz for introducing me to the moving term, "sacred heart."[3] During a sabbatical at the John F. Kennedy School of Government at Harvard University in 2004, I attended Dr. Heifetz's class on leadership. To appreciate his approach, you need to understand that he was not speaking to a group of clergy. In fact, of the 100 people in the class, I was the only professional minister. The rest of the class consisted of people from a variety of vocational professions, faith or no-faith commitments, and various ethnic groups, all of whom were deeply interested in Dr. Heifetz's concept of "adaptive leadership."

Before Heifetz talked about the qualities of adaptive leadership, he saw the need to address the issue of a leader's character. A devout Jew, Heifetz described the "sacred heart" as the capacity for a person in a leadership position to maintain a sense of wonder and awe. When these things are lost, the leader may continue to function, but the joy and excitement fade. Soon, both the leader and the people recognize that everyone is going through the motions, but the meaning has disappeared.

As a follower of Christ, the "sacred heart" had additional meaning for me. In the four Gospels, Jesus spoke often about the intersection of *being* and *doing*. He instructed his disciples on their missional responsibilities. The disciples were called to follow him—to do the works of mercy, teaching, and healing that their Lord did—but they were to act with the same sense of divine presence that Jesus displayed.

In other words, they were committed to *do*, but they were also called to *be*. Unfortunately, we see in the four Gospels, especially the Gospel of Mark, how often the disciples forsook the sacred heart and, in the process, lost sight of their mission. For example, it was difficult for James and John to talk about sacrificial service when they were jockeying for prominent positions in hopes that Jesus would finally bring in the earthly kingdom. Nor was Peter able to maintain any sense of wonder and awe when he was denying that he even knew Jesus.

In these ways, the Bible and especially the four Gospels are vivid reminders of how easy it is for those of us who are church leaders to lose our awe and wonder. We deal with inner struggles to be recognized or face times when opposition makes us afraid, and we respond with pride and fear that supplant any kind of intimate relationship with God or sense of joy in what we are doing.

As a minister, I know how easy it is to become filled with pride and want everyone's accolades. At the same time, I know the fear and anxiety that come when people opposed what I was doing or didn't even like me. Since these seem to be a part of the shared stories of most of us who seek to serve and to lead, the question becomes how to find a spiritual center that gives us the ability to stay focused on what is central to our calling. In the words of Ronald Heifetz, how do we maintain our "sacred heart" even in the middle of the chaos, confusion, and conflict that seem endemic to too many congregations?

While not an overly pious person myself, I have found great help in some of the traditional spiritual practices of the church, such as prayer, meditation, and a reading of the Bible that is informed by the ancient practice of *lectio divina*.[4] These are not all of the classic spiritual practices, but they are the ones I have found most helpful when more negative voices begin to co-opt my "heart."

Anne Lamott, in her earthy, pithy style, writes powerfully about her life of prayer using the stories of her life and her church. One of her recent books has a fascinating title: *Help, Thanks, Wow.* While her works may not be perceived as on level with a study of the giant classics on prayer, such as the works of medieval mystics like Theresa of

Avila, St. Francis, or people in the Benedictine tradition, Lamott has great appeal to many readers because of the way she "popularizes" profound aspects of faith.

Using simple words, Lamott reminds us of essential elements of prayer such as intercession to God for ourselves and others ("help"), gratitude ("thanks"), and a sense of overwhelming awe that God is at work even in the broken places of our lives ("wow").[5]

Meditation

When people envision leadership, they often picture a person who is talking to others in a visionary and motivating way. But where does that speech begin? Do we simply start talking, or are the words formed in the silence where we are open to the nudge of the Divine?

Prayer and meditation are often seen as closely aligned in the Christian tradition, but the two can be different. In his book, *Spirituality for Ministry,* Urban T. Holmes describes the mystical experience that the minister needs before she utters words. Holmes reminds us of the two primary ways that the meditative tradition has developed. In Western Christianity, the *kataphatic* method has been more prominent. This is when a person ponders a certain sacred object or a portion of Scripture and finds focus as well as freedom from the gripping anxieties that are often present in life's ordinary rhythms. For leadership, this means that we are able to speak out of a sense of peace and care rather than being frayed with anxiety.[6]

In the Eastern church, the *apophatic* tradition has prevailed. The goal is to empty the mind and heart, and this is often achieved by the prayerful repetition of a prayer, such as "Jesus Christ, Son of God, Savior, have mercy on me."[7] Again, meditation not only helps us focus on God but also frees us from the stress and tension that undermine our best thinking and our relationships with others.

Reading Holy Scripture

Beginning in 1979, the denomination of which I was a part, the Southern Baptist Convention, went through a terribly divisive time. By the early 1990s, the war was over, and the group labeled the Fundamentalists or Conservatives had triumphed. The agencies, institutions, and seminaries to which many of us were committed are now solidly in the hands of those who identify themselves as biblical literalists or at least believe that the Bible is infallibly the word of God.

Those of us who couldn't support the group's agenda have identified with emerging groups such as the Cooperative Baptist Fellowship, the Alliance of Baptists, or preexisting denominations such as the American Baptist Convention. Perhaps the saddest part of this story for Baptists is that some of the brightest young ministers have connected with other religious groups, their promise lost to the future of Baptists. Other Baptist laypeople and ministers are simply adrift, uncertain about their identity in any group. Some laypeople are still confused about what happened, believing that it was actually a "preacher's fight" that had nothing to do with them.

One tragic casualty in this division of our denomination is that the Bible became a weapon instead of the empowering, inspired document that it is intended to be. Those of us who were labeled "moderates" were accused of not believing the Bible because we didn't interpret every bit of it as literal or historical truth. We have often forgotten what Frederick Buechner wrote: "I believe I have heard my life talk to me if my life talks to me, the way even God talks to me if God talks to me. The language of God seems mostly metaphor."[8]

How does Buechner's idea of Scripture as metaphor relate to leadership? Do I, for instance, have to affirm the historicity of the two differing creation accounts in Genesis 1 and 2 in order to believe that God is ultimately the Creator and Sustainer of life? Personally, I don't feel that I have to reject the preponderance of scientific findings in order to affirm that God is about creating and recreating us. The Hebrew people were exquisite storytellers, and the power of a story is that our lives have plots in which we believe the creating God is always at work, wanting to use us to make our lives and life around us more humane, more just, and more compassionate. This knowledge of God's underlying work gives me strength to try to make a difference for good in the life I live.

Therefore, as a spiritual discipline, the reading of Scripture does several things to empower leadership. First, it reminds us of our identity. We are created by a merciful God whose love extends to us most particularly through God's Son, Jesus Christ. We are energized and led by the Spirit of God. In those times when we don't succeed, we can be reassured by God's love and forgiveness. God does not love conditionally based on our performance and success.

Second, Scripture constantly reminds us that leaders are committed to the poor, the dispossessed, and the marginalized. True leadership is not determined by what we accumulate or by our awards, but by our commitment to make this world a kinder, more caring place.

Third, as leaders employ methods of Scripture reading such as "lectio divina," they understand their own need to be nourished. We don't try to devour large chunks of Scripture with little thought to their meaning; instead, we ponder and pray over smaller sections, hoping that they feed us and give us strength to help others. For example, when we read the agonizing words of Jesus spoken to the people of Jerusalem before his entrance shared in Luke—"If you, even you, had only recognized on this day the things that make for peace!" (Luke 19:41, NRSV)—we have to ask ourselves if we know the things that make for peace in our personal lives.

Leaders are called to articulate powerful concepts to people such as peace, love, hope, courage, and faith. We are asked to help others dream new dreams and envision new possibilities. That is impossible when our own lives are ensnared by fear, anxiety, and the dread that what we say may be rejected. While none of us will internalize those great truths completely, we have to identify what is restraining us from externalizing what we know to be true.

Worship and Community

While there are numerous important disciplines, one that has come to mean so much to me is worship and community. Worship can certainly be done in private. Those moments when we are quiet and "alone with the Alone" give us perspective to approach the noisy, often too busy world in which we live. With the growth of technology, this time alone is even more vitally important. The fact is that most of us are too available, and this will only increase with the progress of technology.

My goal, however, is to emphasize our connections to each other and to God. Worship for me has been difficult. As a preaching minister, I find myself feeling preoccupied with what I'm going to say rather than being moved to recognize the "worth of God" through the great music, prayers, creeds, and confessions of church. To combat this preoccupation with my preaching, I have tried to envision the "sermonic event" as my offering to God. Obviously, I want it to be my best offering, but I have to battle "my best" versus "the best." Every Sunday, I come to the pulpit with the good and bad events of my week, with all the positive and the negative words that I've heard, and always with a sermon that I believe needs a little more work. But I stand in front of the community of faith on Sundays to make my offering to *God*.

After I preach, I go to the door to greet people. Some people are more than gracious in their gratitude for the message. Some folks wish me a good afternoon. A lot of people never come out my door, even though I change doors to try to catch them. Maybe they have to get to lunch. Perhaps they are the kinds of people who have difficulty expressing feelings of appreciation. Or it could be that the offering I gave was not within 100 miles of their needs on that particular day.

When I go to a church meeting, I would love for people to say, "What a wonderful pastor we have!" My ego could use that. But the primary issue for discussion is usually quite different. Once, it was the condition of the furnace in the church basement. Back and forth the congregation argued about whether we should spend money for a new furnace. You would have thought that the furnace was the crux of the kingdom of God.

Does this type of thing bother me? Sure! But I realize several important things simply because I'm getting older. The community of faith has many gracious people. They will commend us even when we, ourselves, may not like our own sermonic offering.

The church also has people who, for whatever reasons, will say nothing to us. We can fret over this, or we can realize that ultimately what we do as ministers is our offering to God. For leadership, this is extraordinarily important. Why we do what we do is vital. If we become preoccupied with those who say nothing and conclude that they don't like us, we will probably have misjudged their reasons for not commenting. Most of all, this attitude will cause discouragement to fester within us and take energy away from what's important.

Finally, most of us deal with some people who are negatively critical of what we do. This is when it's important for us to listen and then to be secure enough to decide what is legitimate criticism and what may come from the critic's own skewed agenda or negative experiences. A good leader listens, but she listens carefully. Some people are never pleased because they're not pleased with themselves. Some are defensive because we may have touched a deep nerve without realizing it. We may look like the uncle who abused her when she was a child. We may remind him of a teacher who said he'd never be good enough. We may sound like their bosses, constantly criticizing them. Leaders must pay attention when a critic's tone of voice or sense of personal attack is out of proportion to the issue. Something else may be underlying the criticism.

Appropriate negative criticism can certainly help us grow and remind us that we always have room to improve as leaders. Above all, we want to avoid feeling badly about ourselves so that, instead of having the capacity to grow, we turn on ourselves and become our own worst critics.[9]

Questions for Reflection

1. Do you believe it is necessary for a leader to possess spiritual qualities? If so, what qualities would you consider most important?

2. Think of someone you know who has a "sacred heart." How does the person reflect that sacred heart in the way he or she lives and leads?

Notes

1. Parker Palmer, *Let Your Life Speak: Listening for the Voice of Vocation* (San Francisco: Jossey-Bass, 2000).

2. Sharon Daloz Parker, *Leadership Can Be Taught: A Bold Approach for a Complex World* (Boston: Harvard Business School Press, 2005).

3. Ronald A. Heifetz and Marty Lewinsky, *Leadership on the Line: Staying Alive Through the Dangers of Leading* (Boston: Harvard Business School Press, 2002) 227–30.

4. Lectio divina is Latin for "divine reading." It is a way to read the Scriptures slowly and meditatively. It has become an increasingly popular way to read Scripture. There are numerous books and articles devoted to helping us read the Bible using this more introspective and potentially life-changing approach. For example, see *Invitation to Christian Spirituality: An Ecumenical Anthology*, ed. John R. Tyson (New York: Oxford University Press), which has several sections devoted to "lectio divina." A more recent book compiled by Matthew Fox, *Christian Mystics: 365 Readings and Mediations* (Novato CA: New World Library, 2011), contains brief statements of leaders throughout the history of the church. These excerpts are designed to help readers ponder them deeply and pray about the implications for their lives.

5. Anne Lamott, *Help, Thanks, Wow: The Three Essential Prayers* (New York: Riverhead Books, 2012).

6. Urban T. Holmes, *Spirituality for Ministry* (San Francisco: Harper and Row Publishers, 1982).

7. Ibid.

8. Frederick Buechner, *The Alphabet of Grace* (New York: Seabury Press, 1970) 13.

9. A much fuller discussion of spiritual disciplines can be found in Richard J. Foster's classic book *Celebration of Discipline: The Path to Spiritual Growth* (New York: Harper and Row, Publishers, 1978). Foster describes thirteen disciplines and divides them into three major categories: the Inward Disciplines, the Outward Disciplines, and the Corporate Disciplines.

Chapter 2

Claiming Ourselves: Leading with Who We Are

An ancient Greek philosopher named Socrates gave us the injunction, "Know thyself." Of course, the Greeks didn't have at their disposal all the assessment tools that we have in the twenty-first century. Now we have tests such as Myers-Briggs that give us insight as to why we act and respond to situations in particular ways.

Through introspection, we examine how we have been nurtured and how that affects both our thinking and our behavior. We begin to understand more clearly our behaviors and the things that make us afraid, sad, joyful, or angry.

Obviously, the feedback of others is essential in trying to know and understand ourselves. That feedback may come from a professional therapist or from people around us whom we trust and hope will give us their honest opinions. A real danger of leadership is to isolate ourselves and not be open to the suggestions or critiques of those who can help us. Because the leader is often the "boss," people may feel intimidated or afraid for their jobs. The leader must work hard to create a culture in which honest feedback is valued and not perceived as disloyalty.

In this chapter, I want to name some of the polarities under which leaders function. Often, books on leadership simply list qualities that a good leader needs. The problem with this approach is that it fails to recognize both the uniqueness of leaders and the fact that most of us are not going to measure up to every quality. Does that eliminate us as leaders? I don't think so.

One of my favorite memories of school is of Recess. I still remember the layout of the schoolyard at Fairlawn Elementary in Miami, Florida. Next to the swing sets were the seesaws or, as some people called them, "teeter-totters." Sometimes, a group of us would spend our entire thirty minutes of recess trying to balance the seesaw. You remember how it goes. One person sits on one end while you try to get somebody of the same approximate weight on the other. Invariably, one is heavier, so the balance shifts in his direction. My best recollection is that we could cram three people on each side. Despite our best efforts, only a few times did we achieve any semblance of balance.

Balance is difficult in leadership as well. In presenting the polarities on leadership, I have two main points. First, none of us achieves perfect balance. You will probably notice, as I do, that there are qualities in which you have some strengths and others that you need to work to develop. With each leadership polarity discussed below, the goal is to recognize and acknowledge our strengths while working on our weaknesses. Sometimes our tendency is to dwell on what we believe we do well while neglecting the other areas. The key to being a good leader, however, is to build all the muscles that are part of a well-rounded leadership configuration.

Listening/Talking

Almost every book or article on leadership identifies clear, cogent communication as essential for a good leader. Frequently, this means a person who is a "good talker."

But what about listening carefully? What about intently observing what is happening around us before we start formulating responses that may have little or nothing to do with the actual situation? In *The Practice of Adaptive Leadership*, Ronald Heifetz, Alexander Grashow, and Marty Linsky write about the three processes that are necessary in their view of leadership: (1) Observe events and patterns around you. (2) Interpret what you observe, developing multiple hypotheses about what is going on. (3) Based on your observations and interpretations, design interventions to address the adaptive challenge you have identified.[1]

Notice what precedes any action or intervention according to Heifetz and his colleagues. It's *observing*, which means careful listening. In the class that I audited with Heifetz at the Kennedy School at Harvard, Heifetz often used the phrase, "listening to the music beneath a person's words." Sometimes we don't tell another person directly what's bothering us. If our listener is carefully tuned both to what we say and the emotive effect of it, however, she may gain our trust and cause us to open up in a deeper way.

The Gospel of John offers some examples of how Jesus listened both to words and especially to the music that exposed the real needs of a person like Nicodemus. On the surface, the conversation that Jesus and Nicodemus have in the third chapter of John seems confusing and convoluted. Nicodemus meets Jesus in a Jerusalem garden at night. We're not told what prompted the encounter. With his outstanding Jewish pedigree and credentials, Nicodemus seems to want to be nice to this young Jewish teacher. "We know that you are a teacher come from God," Nicodemus says, which is high praise for a rabbi from Nazareth in Galilee who, as far as we know, has never attended any rabbinical school.

Thus far, the music of the dialogue is serene. Nicodemus is polite, and we probably expect Jesus to say, "Thank you." But Jesus does not respond to the Jewish leader's compliment. Instead, he tells Nicodemus that he must be "born again" or "born from above," as it's better translated. This sets off a whole exchange in which Nicodemus tries to understand how it is possible to reenter your mother's womb, and Jesus replies that he's talking about a spiritual rebirth.

Is this an example of intense listening on Jesus' part? While most of us would be too polite to identify someone else's need so bluntly, Jesus understood in the context of his ministry what Nicodemus and all of us really need. Politeness never diverted the direction of Jesus' conversations. We hear, as Jesus hears in all of us, the need for a new meaning to our lives.

As we lead any group, the conversation can be loud and confusing. The issue is presented to the members, and some are vocal while others say little if anything. As leaders, can we maintain sufficient distance so that we can hear what is said without becoming embroiled in the emotions? That's absolutely imperative. We have to listen to the content as well as the affective quality of the words that are spoken.

Some people speak loudly because they are afraid of the consequences of a decision. What effect will it have on their power and position? Others are timid and quiet because they believe that their opinions don't merit the time of the group. Any good leader pays careful attention to the silent people because often they may have the best perspectives.

A good leader does not do all the talking herself, and she refuses to allow a few loud voices to dominate the dialogue. Instead, she encourages the value of everyone's contribution to the decision and stresses the importance of listening—both through her own example and through guiding the group to listen to each other. When a decision is finally made, this kind of process allows the best opportunity for everyone to own the decision.

Talking is the other side of the polarity. For some leaders, talking becomes glib and redundant. The meeting room is filled with the sounds of our voices before we've even listened to the people with whom we are working. This style of communication is conveyed by the words, "Here's what I believe! Now what do you think?"

Leadership in a congregation or in any organization certainly requires effective communication. Very little gets done if the person in charge of the meeting says, "Here's the problem. I have no idea what to do. Let's open the floor and share anything that comes to our minds." There are better ways to facilitate decision-making.

First, a leader needs to frame the challenge in ways that people understand. Leaders need to be precise about the issue the group is facing and also make it clear that whatever decision is made will involve some risk. Most decisions encounter some resistance. Many clergy don't like to disturb the equilibrium of the church, and we often wait too long to deal with a problem. I recall a statement by John Claypool, a mentor and pastor to many, saying to me one time, "There is no pleasant way to do unpleasant things."

For example, if the senior pastor is meeting with the personnel committee of the church about an issue involving another staff minister, the senior minister needs to be clear about the problem, have facts to support her position, and prepare a suggested plan of action. For example, should the staff minister be placed on probation or guided to appropriate resources that can help resolve the situation?

Richard Boyatzis and Annie McKee suggest that a leader's primary task is "noticing people's passion and mobilizing the resources of the organization toward the emerging and protean future."[2] Before any leader can do this, he needs to have the confidence and trust of the group. Few things sabotage a leader's intentions more than his lack of focus and preparation.

Second, after framing the issue and presenting the reasons for considering it, the leader needs to listen carefully to the responses of the group. While holding his ground that the challenge he has presented can't be ignored or simply prayed about some more (as important as prayer is), the leader needs to listen in a non-defensive and open manner. Some people on the committee may want to ignore the problem or hope it resolves itself. Through documentation and facts, the leader's task is to keep the group focused on the challenge and to make them realize that this is not a personal vendetta but an issue that ultimately affects the morale and mission of the church.

People on the committee will have good suggestions about how to handle the situation and some ways to make the process work more effectively. It is important to hear the input of these ideas. A good leader desires a decision where the group has ownership, and this rarely happens if only one person's opinion is shared. In that case, none of the group members feel responsibility because none of their ideas have been considered.

Because churches are different, leaders need to work particularly hard in congregations where people tend to be passive and not want to take responsibility. "The pastor has always told us what to do and how to do it," a woman told me once, and I immediately knew that in the interim position I was serving at her church, one of my tasks was to help people find their voices. I could do this best by listening and by talking—taking part in both polarities—at appropriate points along the way.

Passion/Transparency

What is your passion? What do you really want to accomplish? When I was young, I recall a motivational speaker who began his address to a group of us with these questions. The speaker's concept of passion was something that burns within us and drives us to do what we feel is important.

Interestingly, the word "passion" has two almost diametrically opposite meanings. Those of us who are Christians speak of the "Passion" of Jesus. This refers to the events of his crucifixion and his surrender to the Roman authorities. The Passion of the Christ is derived from the same root word from which we get "passive." In other words, Jesus put his life into the hands of others and passively allowed himself to be put to death.

The other way in which "passion" is used refers to the things that inflame us and become the priorities of our lives. Without using the word "passion," Stephen Covey wrote about the "Principles of Personal Vision" in his best-selling book, *The 7 Habits of Highly Effective People.* Covey cited Henry David Thoreau, who also spoke of passion without ever using the word. Thoreau wrote, "I know of no more encouraging thought than the unquestionable ability of Man [sic] to elevate his life by conscious endeavor."[3]

What Thoreau described is a passionate person. This type of leader sees things as they are but is passionate about improving the situation. An excellent example of this type of person is found in the Gospel of Matthew. In the Sermon on the Mount, Jesus made his purpose clear: "Do not think that I have come to abolish the law or the prophets; I have come not to abolish but to fulfill" (Matt 6:17).

As a Jew, Jesus was trained in the Torah and committed to the Jewish laws and precepts. He saw things as they were, and his appreciation for his heritage was deep. At the same time, he sought to enlarge the scope of the Torah and was passionate about calling his listeners to see both the external and internal dimensions of the Law. For instance, when Jesus spoke about the issue of anger, he said,

> You have heard that it was said to those of ancient times, "You shall not murder!"; and whoever murders is liable to judgment. But I say to you that if you are angry with a brother or sister, you will be liable to judgment; and if you insult a brother or sister, you will be liable to the council; and if you say, "You fool," you will be liable to the hell of fire. (Matt 5:21-22)

Obviously, this is more than an objective expansion of a commandment. Jesus feels what he is saying, and while he doesn't reject the Law of Israel, he expands it with great passion. You and I are called to an entirely different way of treating people, and the consequences of disobedience expand Jesus' commitment to the Torah of the Old Covenant.

While passion for a cause motivates us to act and to try to change things, that passion may easily slip into a leader's abuse of power. We may feel so strongly about something that we cease to be open to differing opinions. Our passion becomes an expression of power, and that sense of power may drive us to eliminate dissenting voices. We feel so strongly about an issue that it leads us to silence or even to get rid of people who stand in the way of our exercise of power.

Jeffrey Pfeffer, the Thomas D. Dee II Professor of Organizational Behavior at the Stanford University Graduate School of Business, wrote an intriguing article for the *Harvard Business Review* titled, "Power, Capriciousness, and Consequences." Pfeffer pointed out the potentially negative consequences of passion turned into power: "Over the course of millennia, a heuristic association between eschewing behavioral norms and possessing power: We observe that powerful people are able to ignore what's expected and to do what they please."[4]

In order for passion not to become power—to balance the polarity between the two—a leader must maintain transparency to others. The biblical term for this transparency is "humility." Humility does not mean that we are always waffling and changing our positions. In fact, there are times when the leader needs to hold steady and to recognize that he's not going to get universal support. But, regardless of disagreement or conflict, a leader needs to respect others, maintain his composure, be aware of and manage his emotions, and not become part of a shouting match. One of the worst things that can happen is when the issue is forgotten in a flood of rage or name-calling.

M. Craig Barnes remembers his graduation from Princeton Theological Seminary and the moving address given to the graduates by Father Henri Nouwen. Nouwen used the phrase "downward mobility." He was speaking to a group of bright, ambitious students who were eager to take their gifts and education and change the world, achieve some degree of fame, and certainly become "upwardly mobile" as they achieved greater recognition.

What Nouwen said sliced against the grain of how most of us approach life. Speaking of ministry, Nouwen challenged these seminary graduates as he challenges many of us: "It means the road of downward mobility in the midst of an upwardly mobile world. I do not say this with sadness, but joyfully, because the downward road of God is the road on which he reveals himself to us as God with us."[5]

As Barnes reflected after a season in the parish, he perceptively wrote his own description of "downward mobility":

> Most ministers nurture a cherished self-image of being Moses, trying to lead God's people to the Promised Land. We like to think we can get there somewhere. But I am amazed at how much time we spend wandering around in the desert. I have had the same conversation about the youth group eating pizza in the church parlor at least two hundred times, in three different churches, since I have been ordained. I spend an enormous amount of my time, not holding trembling hands, but paying the rent. I am convinced that the church is different because of my presence, but I am not convinced it is any closer to the Promised Land. I am willing to risk being a failure for Jesus, and I can certainly handle success. But the one journey I didn't want to take was the daily meandering of God's people. That, however, is where I am called. And I am absolutely convinced this is the only way the love of Jesus is going to make sense to my parishioners.[6]

For every leader in the church, there must be balance between passion and transparency. When I look at myself, I realize that I don't change as much or as quickly as I may like. I still want to keep the challenge of being different and, hopefully, a better follower of Christ. I don't want to settle for meandering in the mediocre. At the same time, I'm dealing with people like me. We never want to stop calling people to the promised land, but we want to be aware that it is a desert journey for all of us.

Getting What We Want/Learning to Lose Gracefully

One of my favorite writers on leadership is Bill George, former chair and CEO of the company Medtronics. While much of George's writing is addressed to the corporate world, he does have some important points that speak to the church. George is a strong and vocal advocate of "value-driven leadership." For example, he stated, "Authentic companies value the importance of stewardship to the people they serve—customers, employees, shareholders, and communities. They measure their success by the extent to which they fulfill the needs and desires of those diverse communities."[7]

George's comment raises the vital issue of what a company or corporation values most. Let's look at a church for a moment. While churches differ in the things they value most and even state some of what are essentially the same values in various ways, it's important for congregations to articulate their fundamental values.

Imagine a congregation that is seeking a new pastor. In the Baptist tradition, a search committee is elected and, with the input of the congregation, the committee develops a profile of the qualities they desire in their new minister. Usually, the ability to preach, pastoral care skills, and administrative or leadership abilities top the list. Some churches that have developed a strong community image will look for a pastor who relates to the various faith communities and communal structures that are a part of the sphere of the church.

Now, try to decide precisely what each quality means to the search committee, never mind the entire congregation. "I want a good preacher," one member says. But what is meant by "good preacher"? Does Sue mean the same things as John, who also wants a "good preacher"?

Let's ask Sue what a "good preacher" is. She responds, "She's poised, connects to the listeners with her eyes and presence, doesn't read the sermon, and always makes sure that she issues a clear invitation to nonbelievers to know Jesus as their personal Savior and Lord." Ask Sue if that means the intent of every sermon is evangelistic. "Not exactly," Sue says. "The sermon should help people in the church grow in their relationship with Jesus Christ, but it also should make clear how people can begin a relationship with Christ."

It's John's turn to speak. Sue and John are on the same committee, and both of them are looking for an effective preacher. Are Sue and John looking for the same things? John says, "I'm looking for real substance. I don't care whether the preacher ever looks at me. I want the sermon to be well-crafted, and I prefer that he reads the whole thing so he stays on course.

"Furthermore," John says, "whether the church grows is irrelevant to me. I want a preacher who tackles the social issues that are affecting our society. What about war, discrimination, and bias toward people whose sexual preference is different from mine? I have a friend at work who is gay. He doesn't have a church that welcomes and embraces him. I want a good preacher who is courageous enough to address these controversial issues."

Both Sue and John want an effective preacher, but I predict some "banging of heads" on their way to the "Reverend Good-Speak." Conflict is endemic to churches because people disagree on the many components of church life. Churches with congregational forms of governance are especially susceptible to conflict. Styles of worship are particularly contentious these days, and some people even refer to them as "worship wars." Social issues are also a deep concern for congregations and denominations. For example, consider "John's" gay friend who was looking for a church that would accept him as he is. Try bringing up this issue in some congregations, and witness the hostility. People take sides, and everybody, no matter what his position, invokes the Bible and God. It's hard to argue with God and the Bible, particularly when they seem to be on everybody's side.

What makes these concerns even more difficult is that they become win-lose propositions. I realize the difficulty of finding consensus on many issues, and I also recognize that we have convictions about various issues. Obviously, there are no easy solutions or quick fixes to issues that a church faces. However, the words of Bill George may help us to get along and stay together even if we're not all singing the same song. "Authentic companies value the importance of stewardship to the people they serve," he wrote. "They measure their success by the extent to which they fulfill the needs and desires of their diverse communities."[8]

While we all have convictions about various issues, it is easy to allow our disagreements to make us lose sight of the fundamental reason for the church's existence. As the body of Christ, we are called in our diversity to serve the living Christ and to serve all whom God loves. Our task is not to win every vote and have the church follow our wishes. We are called to serve, and that means we may lose the vote on some issues. If losing causes us to withdraw or become angry and resentful, then we have lost the most important thing: a heart for God.

Introspective/Team Building

In terms of personality traits, most leader types are comfortable with groups of people and enjoy the task of "team building." But what about the other side of this polarity, which I've called "introspective"? What about the need for us to be still, to meditate, to contemplate, and to decide within ourselves what is central and where we should direct our best efforts?

In the early 1980s, Daniel Stoop wrote a book with the eye-catching title, *You Are What You Think.* While Stoop's work predicted some of the important research on systems' theory and emotional intelligence, he also dealt in a practical way with important issues such as how we think and talk to ourselves. Most of us are familiar with "self-talk." The internal conversations that we have shape our attitudes and behaviors.

What led Stoop to discuss our self-talk is something he labeled, "I am what I think." Consider Stoop's reasoning:

> The title is that our emotions and behavior are *not* dependent on what is going on around us in our environment. . . . The reason is that something else is at work that determines emotional and behavioral responses to life situations. The cognitive theorists suggest that this additional factor is our thoughts or belief systems.[9]

Essentially, team building is trying to shape a system of people, to build their morale, and to accomplish a mission. Obviously, every person in the system is wired in a different way. There are also subsystems within the bigger system.

If we are the leaders, we introduce ourselves into the amalgam of all these systems. And by doing that, we introduce another system—ourselves—into an already complex equation. Nobody ever said leadership was easy, unless we are dealing with robots or with people who have been brainwashed to follow and not to speak their minds.

I'm not for robotic or brainwashing leadership, so let's recognize that we have a challenge. If you are a leader in a church, you know how difficult it is to get people focused on a task. If anything is going to be accomplished, however, the leader must have made the journey inward and found the resources in prayer and in her relationship to God that will keep her steady in the face of negative criticism and resistance to a sense of mission. If the leader is frayed and angry, then the whole discussion becomes interpersonal, and the focus on commitment to mission is lost in the battle of "I'm right; you're wrong."

Intellectually Alert/Emotionally Awake

Most of us with the benefit of a good education have had our minds prepared to think and to process problems. The tests we have taken either to get into a school or to measure our progress in a class were designed to measure our intelligence and ability to solve problems. For the most part, at least in my experience, academia was planned to stretch the mind and to measure what we know.

The Intelligence Quotient (IQ) tests that we have taken are intended to measure such things as our verbal and mathematical skills. Obviously, nothing is wrong with measuring our IQ or recognizing the importance of these skills. Most leaders are smart, although they may not be the smartest people in the organization. They are skilled enough, however, to think through the challenges that the group is facing and to understand both the substance and the nuances of the problem.

Within the last two decades, a complementary tool to measure leadership skills (other than IQ) has emerged in academic circles. While not demeaning the importance of intelligence as a component of leadership, this new way of looking at how organizations and groups function emphasizes the importance of Emotional Quotient (EQ). After all, each of us is more than a mind. We do more than think about issues. While cognitive abilities are important, all of us have seen individuals in group settings who have hurt themselves and others by becoming enraged over something. When that happens, the focus of the meeting is often completely lost.

Daniel Goleman has written prolifically about EQ. In a book he coauthored with Richard Boyatzis and Anne McGee about resonant leaders, a synonym for emotionally mature leaders, he said,

> Resonant leaders know when to be collaborative and when to be visionary, when to listen and when to command. Since leaders have a knack for attending to their own sense of what matters and articulating a mission that resonates with the values of those they lead, these leaders naturally nurture relationships, surface simmering issues, and create the human synergies of a group in harmony.[10]

Often the qualities of emotional intelligence are communicated in an open-box form under the headings "Personal Competence" and "Social Competence." Personal Competence is how we manage ourselves, and Social Competence is the way we determine how we manage relationships. The box may look something like this:[11]

Personal Competence
Self-awareness
Emotional Self-awareness: reading one's emotions and recognizing their impact.

Accurate self-assessment: knowing one's strengths and weaknesses.

Self-confidence: a sound sense of one's self-worth and capabilities.

Social Competence
Social Awareness
Empathy: seeing others' emotions, understanding their perspectives, and taking active interest in their concerns.

Organizational Awareness: reading the currents, dynamics, and politics at the organizational level.

Service: recognizing and meeting followers', clients', or customers' needs.

Personal Competence

Self-management

Emotional Self-control: keeping disruptive emotions under control.

Transparency: displaying honesty and integrity; trustworthiness.

Achievement: the drive to improve performance to meet inner standards of excellence.

Initiative: readiness to act and seize opportunities.

Optimism: seeing the upside in events.

Social Competence

Relationship Management

Inspirational Leadership: creating and motivating with a compelling vision.

Influence: wielding a range of tactics for persuasion.

Developing Others: bolstering others' abilities through feedback and guidance.

Change Catalyst: initiating, managing, and leading in a new direction.

Conflict Management: resolving disagreements.

Teamwork and Collaboration: cooperation and team building.

Taking Time for Ourselves/Giving Our Best to Our Callings

Those of us who were students at the Southern Baptist Theological Seminary in the late 1960s and early 1970s had the privilege to know and be influenced by Wayne Oates. Oates was a pioneer in the field of pastoral care and theology. A prolific author, he was largely responsible for the field of pastoral care being accepted as a recognized theological discipline.

In the early 1990s, shortly before I left the faculty of Southern Seminary, I had the privilege of serving as interim pastor for Dr. Oates and his wife Pauline at St. Matthew's Baptist Church in Louisville. In one sense, it was a "scary" privilege. After I accepted the call to be interim, I told my wife, "Diane, what am I going to say in a sermon that Wayne Oates doesn't already know or hasn't probably written about in a book or article?" That presumes that what I was saying in a sermon would have been critical enough to make it into Oates's writings.

What I found in Wayne and Pauline Oates was a generosity of spirit that I've found in many accomplished people who are secure within themselves. Hardly a Sunday passed that both of them didn't come out my door following worship and thank me for the message. In fact, Wayne Oates paid me the ultimate compliment when he wrote the preface to a book I had written about our son's illness, *Learning to Dream Again.* Oates recalled a sermon I had preached on the woman taken in adultery and complimented me for what he termed my "imaginative approach" to that story. Frankly, as a preacher, I could live on those kind words for the rest of my ministry.

Among the many books that Wayne Oates authored was *Confessions of a Workaholic.*[12] Published in 1971, *Confessions* became a best-seller and actually created a new word, "workaholic," that later made it into the *Oxford English Dictionary.* Oates shared his own journey to find balance between work and play in his life. Obviously, he had given his best to his calling and helped to shape a whole theological discipline in the process. But what about relaxation and play? Just as someone becomes addicted to a substance, Oates had become addicted to his work. Thus he called himself a "workaholic."

Effective leaders have great demands on their time and energy. People look to them for insight and guidance. Often, it's hard to say "no" when you feel that you are needed and can make a contribution. The problem is that constantly saying "yes" can leave a person feeling depleted, frustrated, and even depressed. If a leader has a family, their needs are ignored, and the sole purpose of life becomes trying to fix every problem and solve every issue. When work becomes the rudder that guides the ship of ourselves, it becomes an addiction.

Somehow, the balance must be found between our work and whatever we do to play or to relax. This is particularly important as a leader ages. When we get older, two things usually happen that can be devastating if our sense of self has been built on achievement. First, we are not in demand as much as we once were. The question is, "Can we move into a new season of life without the telephone ringing, the emails coming, and the constant texts that are asking us to do something for somebody else?"

The second issue is our diminishing sense of energy and, perhaps, some physical limitations. Fortunately, I have had good health, but I am discovering that my body is not the same at seventy as is was at forty. When I go to the physician now, my doctor usually prefaces his remarks with, "At your age . . . ." I know how old I am, but sometimes I forget that at my age, there are parts of my body that ache, and I didn't even know I had these body parts thirty years ago.

How vital it is for us to build and to nurture relationships with family and friends. These are the lasting components of a life well led. Wayne Oates has reminded us of a powerful concept—how easy it is for those of us who like to lead and who want to be recognized for what we've accomplished to be seduced by our work and spend our lives looking for the next fix. Working to balance this polarity is essential for being a good leader.

Questions for Reflection

1. What other polarities of leadership would you add to those described in this chapter?

2. When you look at yourself, which of the qualities would you consider your strengths? Which would be areas where you might grow?

3. Do you believe leaders are born, or can they be developed?

Notes

1. Ronald Heifetz, Alexander Grashow and Marty Linsky, *The Practice of Adaptive Leadership: Tools and Tactics for Changing Your Organization and the World* (Boston: Harvard Business Press, 2009) 32.

2. Richard Boyatzis and Annie McGee, *Resonant Leadership: Remembering Yourself and Connecting with Others Through Mindfulness, Hope, and Compassion* (Boston: Harvard Business School Press, 2005) 10.

3. Stephen R. Covey, *The 7 Habits of Highly Effective People: Restoring the Character* (New York: Free Press, 1989) 66.

4. Jeffrey Pfeffer, "Power, Capriciousness, and Consequence," *Harvard Business Review*, April 2013, p. 36.

5. Henri Nouwen, cited in M. Craig Barnes, *When God Interrupts: Finding New Life through Undaunted Change* (Downer's Grove IL: Intervarsity Press, 1996) 47.

6. Barnes, *When God Interrupts*, 48–49.

7. Bill George, *Authentic Leadership: Rediscovering the Secrets to Creating Lasting Value* (San Francisco: Jossey-Bass, 2003) 71.

8. Ibid., 71.

9. David Stoop, *You Are What You Think* (Grand Rapids MI: Fleming H. Revell, 1982) 28.

10. Daniel Goleman, Richard Boyatzis, and Annie McKee, *Primal Leadership: Recognizing the Power of Emotional Intelligence* (Boston: Harvard Business Press, 2013) 48.

11. Ibid., appendix 2, 253–56.

12. Wayne Oates, *Confessions of a Workaholic: The Facts about Work Addiction* (New York: World Pub. Co., 1971).

Chapter 3

The Changing Faces of Church Leadership

When I taught preaching, I heard a fellow preacher describe the evolution of homiletics. In many of our faith traditions thirty or forty years ago, preaching ministers were almost all male. In seminaries or divinity schools where most if not all of the students were white males, the professor would pick a model preacher such as Phillips Brooks, who had been rector of Trinity Church in Boston and also chaplain at Harvard Divinity School.

The primary aim of the teacher was to get students to imitate Brooks, who was known as a masterful proclaimer. Students studied Brooks, his methods of preparing a sermon, and his style of delivery. The professor's intention was to get the students to emulate Brooks in every respect. The way to be an outstanding preacher was to study a masterful preacher, and the students tried to get as close to that as possible.

Fortunately, driven by two primary forces, the vast majority of schools have discarded this approach to teaching homiletics. One force is the recognition that people are gifted in different ways, and the task of teaching is to call out the gifts that students have and try to refine those gifts. The task is not to put any of us in someone else's ill-fitting armor, as Saul tried to do with young David in 1 Samuel.

The second, perhaps even more important force is the increasing diversity of people who feel the call to ministry. In many of the classes I taught, a majority of the students were often women. While I tried to listen to my students, get input from women who taught homiletics in other institutions, and use textbooks written by women, I realized that, as a white male, I was always dealing with my own nature and nurture. Empathy can go a long way, but it hardly qualifies any of us to say about someone else, "I know exactly what you're feeling."

Making the transition to leadership means entering largely uncharted waters. We want to avoid the oversimplification that all men lead a certain way, and all women lead another way. This is not only an oversimplification; it also creates a bias that *all* men and *all* women lead in different ways. Regardless of gender, good leaders share particular attributes. Instead of trying to emphasize differences, we may need to try to understand each other first, to appreciate the qualities that all good leaders seem to possess, and then to learn from each other.

In this chapter, I will try to offer a perspective on women as leaders. I realize this doesn't take into account the different leadership styles of those in churches of various ethnic and racial groups. I will leave that to people who know far more about these unique characteristics than I do. I simply want to encourage us to recognize that, with all our cultural diversity, there are myriad approaches to leadership.

More important, since this is my perspective, I hope it will encourage women in the church to write about their approaches to leadership so that older white men like me can be corrected and helped to understand better. The corporate world is witnessing a rise of women in leadership positions, and the church needs to be ready for women not only to have a seat on the front of the bus but also to drive it. I applaud denominations that have opened the door to women as pastors. I'm grateful in my Baptist tradition for the leadership of wise, courageous folks like Dr. Pam Durso and for organizations like Baptist Women in Ministry, which Pam leads. We are further behind other groups, but we are trying to catch up. I regularly meet women with outstanding gifts who give me hope that we are on the front end of a new day.

Below, I will discuss qualities that are usually identified as "feminine." This doesn't mean that only women possess them, but they are often associated with attributes that we have placed under the rubric of "feminine." At the same time, I want to remind myself again that, as a male, the worst thing I can do is to diminish the God-given temperaments and talents that many people possess that fit into no category. With this caveat, let's analyze some qualities that are essential for effective leadership and that traditionally have been thought of as feminine.

Assertive

This quality may sound surprising when we think about leadership qualities, especially those labeled as "feminine." Like many of you, I grew up in a culture where people were expected to "know their places" as defined by gender, race, and capabilities. When I tell my children, for example, that I remember how people of color were forced to use separate bathrooms, eat at different restaurants, live in segregated neighborhoods, and go to schools where everyone was African American, my children are astounded and angry.

Fortunately, much of that "Jim Crow" attitude has changed, and now people of color have more opportunities. At times, we see the sordid specter of prejudice, and we realize that while progress has been made, Martin Luther King Jr.'s eloquent dream of the "promised land" has not been fully realized.

I also grew up in a gender gap that was usually presented in a more benign way. Television shows like *Father Knows Best* and *Ozzie and Harriet* projected the image that a man's place was to go to work while his spouse stayed home, making sure that supper was fixed and that she greeted her husband wearing a dress, high heels, and a smile as she said, "I hope you had a good day." Perhaps Ozzie reciprocated and asked Harriet if she liked being stuck at home all day, but I don't remember his doing that.

Leave it to Beaver was another show that reinforced the stereotype. Everybody seemed happy with his or her place, and if the children had problems, they were minor and usually handled by a family conference that was headed, of course, by Dad. Suppose June Cleaver had said to her husband, "Ward, you stay home and take care of Beaver and Wally. Have supper ready when I get back from work. Skip the high heels, but wear an ironed shirt and suit!" Frankly, in the 1950s, most of us would have fallen off our chairs. Role reversal was certainly not in my vocabulary.

But times are changing—though not quickly enough—and I have found in my own daughter and in countless female students in my classes an unwillingness to stay in some place that somebody has told them is a woman's role. Some women have been angry about it. Others have turned their passivity into appropriate assertiveness. Like Rosa Parks, they refuse to sit in the back of anybody's bus and want to exercise freely the gifts that God has given them.

While Sheryl Sandberg is not a leader in the life of the church, this chief operating officer of Facebook has given a powerful voice to women who want their places at the table of leadership. In her best-selling book, *Lean In: Women, Work, and the Will to Lead*, she wrote,

> There's no doubt that women have the skill to lead in the workplace. Girls are increasingly outperforming boys in the classroom, earning about 57% of the undergraduate and 60% of the Master's degrees in the United States. This gender gap in academic achievement has even caused some to worry about the "end of men." But while compliant, raise-your-hand-and-speak-when-called-on behaviors might be rewarded in school, they are less valued in the workplace. Career progression often depends upon taking risks and advocating for oneself—traits that girls are discouraged from exhibiting.[1]

Many of us in the church, including both women and men, need to understand that assertiveness comes from the confidence that God gives us. The Bible is replete with stories of women who took risks, got to the tomb of Jesus first, and provided leadership in the early church. Assertiveness doesn't preclude humility, because to be in Christ (as the Apostle Paul often said) is to know the security of whose we are and who we are.

We can be assertive without being overbearing or shrill. We can exhibit confidence without falling off the ledge of cockiness. Why not include assertiveness as both a feminine and masculine trait, and then bless it as a virtue? In our congregations today with plummeting attendance, fewer young people, and diminishing resources, there is a desperate need for leaders to take risks for the good of all.

Relational

Again, it's a stretch to say that women leaders are always more relational while men tend to be autocratic and operate from the top down. Things are changing, and now most leadership books caution against the autocratic type of leadership that conveys, "I have the corner on all wisdom."

When I was teaching homiletics, I noticed a difference between many of the women and men who preached. Because of our Baptist tradition in the South, many of the women had never preached before. There was almost a beautiful tentativeness in their approach to the sermon. This was especially evident when their text was a narrative piece of Scripture. They allowed us to experience the text rather than racing to tell us the points of the message. Listening to them was like going on a journey in which they walked beside us as fellow travelers and helpful guides. We heard the rhythm of the text and were able to draw out messages for ourselves. This is relational preaching, and it's akin to relational leadership. In effect, the leader walks with us as a sojourner and guide. She treats us as people who have minds of our own and respects our insights.

Norma Cook Everist and Craig Nessan underscore this point in their book, *Transforming Leadership*:

> As one leads with authority and people live unto trusting the person who occupies the office, steadily one moves from relying primarily on the "formal" authority of the office to gaining "acknowledged" authority. *Formal authority* is what people are willing to ascribe to one based on the office one holds. *Acknowledged authority* is based on the trustworthiness and skill one has demonstrated in building solid relationships with the people one serves.[2]

The authors' observations on authority are important to note. Those who have seen authority abused and twisted into authoritarianism sometimes back off from appropriate use of authority. Relational leaders strive for the egalitarian approach where everyone's voice can be heard, and each person in the congregation or church is respected. That doesn't mean, however, that the leader should shy away from voicing his opinions or taking the risk of trying to give direction and guidance to other people. We shouldn't impose our views, but neither should we want our voices to be muted because we're afraid of rejection or being perceived as a top-down leader.

These days, churches seem to be struggling with leaders who are too authoritarian or with so-called leaders who are afraid to voice their convictions. A balance is essential. At their best, churches are usually awkward in terms of how decisions are made and in identifying the people who can exercise appropriate power and make things happen.

While there are no magic bullets to make everything in the church as symmetrical and as high functioning as we may like, a relational leader who exercises appropriate authority remembers the need for wisdom, compassion, and a sense of self that is not based on having everything go his or her way.

Spiritual Awareness

Are women more aware than men of the need for dependence on God? That's debatable because we all know genuinely pious men who do the work of the church. Yet my sense from years as a minister is that more often than not, women reflect not just activity in the life of the church but also greater attention to their inner lives. I'm indebted to Professor Robert C. Solomon of the University of Texas at Austin, who has helped me try to define the illusive word "spirituality."[3] While I don't agree with everything Solomon says, he provides thoughtful insights about the nature of spirituality.

Spirituality is different from religion. Religion is often sectarian and can promote the attitude, "My religion is better than yours." When viewed like this, religion is divisive, separating us from each other in our shared humanity. The most elemental New Testament verse, "For God so loved the world . . ." (John 3:16), is shattered by distrust, suspicion, and even outright hatred. We love only those who think our way, speak our religious language, and mirror our constricted viewpoints on issues. This kind of religion becomes a hammer to attack others, and the idea of God's loving the "whole world" is jettisoned as we attack those who don't agree with us.

Generally speaking, women seem to be better negotiators, more willing to listen to the ideas of those with whom they disagree and to find some common ground of consensus. On the other hand, the masculine part of us wants to be aggressive, to dominate, and to win. We battle vigorously for propositions and positions and often think little about the person whom we are trying to defeat.

In fundamentalist religions and highly partisan political positions that are dominated by male leadership, people react to their adversaries with a win/lose mentality. The result is that they fail to see each other as good creations of God, and they respond by trying to marginalize or even eliminate those who don't share their "right" points of view.

When I was a child, I recall that my church and every other church I was aware of depended on women to keep things functioning. Of course, at that point women couldn't hold positions of authority such as pastor or deacon, but they planned most of the activities, cooked the food, served the tables, and cleaned up with very little thanks. In some ways, today this sounds demeaning to women. But I still wonder what motivated them to give themselves to their understanding of service to God. Did they act out of submission? Did they feel that they wanted to serve God, and this was all they could do? I'm sure both of these reasons and more were true when it came to motives for service. As a child, however, I remember talking with women who seemed to have a deep spiritual awareness and who eagerly sought any way to serve God and to set the example for those of us who were watching.

Elsie Miller taught a group of fourth grade boys at my church. She was famous for her patience and her heavenly deviled eggs. Frankly, we were an awful class for Mrs. Miller. We were more interested in baseball and were beginning to ask why all our classes were separated by gender. Despite our less than Christ-like behaviors, Mrs. Miller plowed on with her lessons and usually ended them by telling each of us that God loved us. It didn't seem to make a difference at the time, but in retrospect, I still hear Elsie Miller saying, "Chuck, God loves you."

Elsie was part of a generation of women who would never have entertained the ideas of going to seminary to become pastors or of being elected as deacons in their churches. Little did she know how much she helped me to appreciate the spiritual depth of women on whose shoulders later generations of women would stand. These later generations are now able to be leaders in ways that Elsie probably never imagined.

To make a quantum generation leap, I recently came across an insightful book, *Giving 2.0*, written by Laura Arrillaga-Andreesson.[4] Her topic reminds me of Elsie Miller, a woman of modest means who later gave me my first personal Bible and was always encouraging others with thoughtful gifts.

Arrillaga-Andreesson writes to people who have the means to invest in programs to help the poor and oppressed and to start foundations that help the needy and dispossessed. She tells the stories of some men, but mostly of women who have done significant entrepreneurial work to give to others. Her book awakens our spiritual awareness to people with resources who should use what they have to help others. In many cases, someone with spiritual passion simply needed to ask these people to develop channels for their giving. Once they had the motivation and were aware of the need, they were happy to share their resources.

Both women and men with a deep concern for the poor, the hungry, and those who need the basic resources of life will find this book valuable for helping them access the amount of financing that can make a significant difference.

Empathy

Empathy is the ability to feel the joys and pains of those around us. When I taught preaching, I heard Tom Long, the outstanding Professor of Preaching at Candler School of Theology at Emory University, make a profound observation about what he had discerned as a difference between many female and male students. As Long listened to student sermons, he discerned the ability of many women to enter a biblical text and feel the emotions of the characters in a story. For example, in Jesus' parable of the prodigal son, the older brother wasn't merely a self-centered workaholic who only wanted parties thrown in his honor.

Think about it! He stayed home. He didn't ask for his inheritance before his father died. Nobody had to tell the older son to do his work. Maybe he was too rigid. Perhaps he thought that if he acted dutifully and morally, he should be recognized. But almost every sermon I've ever heard on this story paints the good son as the villain and the wayward son as a victim who deserved the ring, the robe, and the fatted calf.

The parable is actually stunning in its role reversal, and we may not get close to the heart of God if we don't see the twist. The best way to proclaim this parable is to live into the story, empathize with the father and both sons, and then be amazed by the grace that always writes surprising endings to the sagas of our lives.

In his insightful way, Long traced the female adult's ability to empathize back to the ways that a group of boys and a group of girls interact as children. In a group of boys, if somebody has a problem, answers are immediately offered to solve the problem. In a group of girls, however, they are much more likely to begin with words of comfort and then to collaborate on ways to help a wounded friend.

While times have certainly changed since I was playing in the schoolyard, I noticed the same empathetic strains in many of the women I taught. It's not that they couldn't be decisive. After all, many of them were spurred by a sense of strength and a sense of transcendent calling that brought them to a vocation that still had far more job openings for males only. In terms of leadership, though, empathy expresses itself in concern for the welfare of those with whom the leader is working. This type of leader sees people as more than just staff or employees. She listens carefully to their joys and needs so that each of them feels important.

Empathy does not mean that there aren't times for appropriate confrontation. The best kind of love is not an oozy feeling that lets people get by without doing their best. Instead, it cares enough about others to call the very best out of them.

Some leaders are afraid of any kind of emotional closeness because they are fearful that it will make them too vulnerable and open to manipulation. Obviously, that's always a risk, and a good leader needs to be astute in recognizing that caring for people requires appropriate boundaries. Dr. Wayne Oates, one of the early leaders in the pastoral care movement, said to my fellow students and me in a seminary class one day, "If you become a pastor, make sure that you are close enough to your congregation so they feel your warmth, but have enough distance so that when they come to you with a need, they feel that they have gone somewhere."

Confidence

Once in a while, I get an email or letter from a woman who was a student of mine, and she thanks me for helping her to be confident enough to find her voice. Notes like that from former students mean the world to me because I'm not sure that a professor does anything more important than instilling confidence in a student. Of course, that's not a universal experience. Some students come into class on the first day saying, "I can't do this," and they leave the final class still saying, "I can't do this!" But the light bulb does come on for some students, and the real meaning of confidence, "filled with faith," shines forth.

By no means has our society, much less many of our churches, made sufficient progress toward the full recognition of the gifts of women. Corporate structures, political systems, and religious institutions are still largely dominated by men. Some progress has been made but hardly enough. Some religious denominations have become more open to women as leaders, but many of us still have miles to go.

I want to encourage the women whom I know and countless others whom I don't know to continue the struggle. I know that it's easy for me as a white male to say this, but I've heard too many of you preach in the most moving ways. I've watched you lead with vision and passion when given the opportunity. You have so much to offer.

I wish I could throw wide the doors of opportunity for you. I pray that the walls that sometimes keep you from fulfilling your God-inspired dreams will come tumbling down. When my daughter called me a number of years ago to say that she wanted to attend divinity school, I still remember what I said: "Laura Beth, you have chosen a difficult road simply because you are a woman. But your dad could not be prouder of you for the road you are taking." If I could sit down with each of you, I would say the same thing.

Be confident. Be filled with faith. I couldn't be prouder of you.

Questions for Reflection

1. What qualities of leadership would you list as traditionally masculine or feminine?

2. What can female and male leaders learn from each other?

3. If you are a woman, what types of things would you say to other women to encourage them as leaders?

Notes

1. Sheryl Sandberg with Nell Scovell, *Lean In: Women, Work, and the Will to Lead* (New York: Alfred A. Knopf, 2013) 15.

2. Norma Cook Everist and Craig L. Nessan, *Transforming Leadership: New Vision for a Church in Mission* (Minneapolis: Fortress Press, 2008) 60.

3. Robert C. Solomon, "The Passions: Philosophy and the Intelligence of Emotions," audiotape produced by the Teaching Company, part 2, disc 12, tape 24.

4. Laura Arrillaga-Andreesson, *Giving 2.0* (San Francisco: Jossey-Bass, 2012).

Chapter 4

Styles of Leadership

Most of us who find ourselves in positions of leadership have a primary approach to doing what we do. While our way of leadership may vary depending on such things as the critical nature of the situation or the maturity level of the people with whom we work, we usually gravitate to the style of leadership that is comfortable for us.

Our preferred way of leading is influenced by our nature, our experiences in life, and a host of other factors of which we may not be consciously aware. In the life of the church, our theology may affect the way we lead. For example, in some seminaries, a more autocratic style is taught, and portions of Scripture that speak about the clergy being "head" of the church are invoked. Conversely, other schools emphasize a more democratic or relational style of leadership. Once again, texts in the Bible that seem to support this approach are brought to the witness stand for evidence.

When we address styles of leadership, we have the resources of numerous books and articles that advocate a certain approach. Complicating this is the fact that there are nuanced approaches to most of the major styles of leadership. Thus, it's impossible to cover all the various styles, particularly since leadership is an art where new ideas appear constantly.

I will begin with four primary leadership styles that are discussed in John Jackson and Lorraine Bosse'-Smith's book, *Leveraging Your Leadership Style.* Then, I will address several other approaches that have gained some following.

Jackson and Bossé-Smith name four styles of leadership: the Commander, the Coach, the Counselor, and the Conductor.

The Commander

Commanders are quick to make decisions, set visions for an organization, and are often driven in what they want to achieve.

Commanders are not afraid to take risks, and they face the future with anticipation and not fear. If you are a commander, you may be sought for your leadership in a crisis situation.

Commanders are not the most relationally skilled people, however, and they have little or no concern about being liked or being friends with their coworkers. They have to be careful when they work with people who have other leadership styles. Commanders assume that they are right about decisions and have the correct vision for the group. They often find it difficult to listen to opposing voices.[1]

Commanders must also be cautious in taking all the responsibility on themselves. In times of crisis, people tend to look for a savior to lead them, but then they begin to resent that they have surrendered the shape of their future to one person. This often occurs in churches that are going through difficult times. The church calls a pastor to take responsibility for its survival, but once the church achieves firm footing, some members begin to resent that they have no say in the shaping of the group's future. A "commander" type of leader is wise to recognize when the crisis passes and to realize that responsibility for leadership should be spread to a larger number of people.

The Coach

Coaches are enthusiastic leaders who work well with teams or groups of people. While leaders who function as coaches tend to be persuasive in communication, they need to avoid the negativity that comes when every situation is viewed as win/lose.

Obviously, people on the team need to function at a high level. Therefore, it's appropriate for leaders to make suggestions and encourage better performance. In sharing this criticism, however, coaches should be mindful of the needs of each person and not simply project their frustrations on those whom they perceive to be underperforming. Win/lose leaders expect much of themselves and others. While high expectations start out as positive, they become negative when the compulsion to excel causes us to treat others as well as ourselves in negative ways.

Coach ministers are usually effective in the work of the church. They want things to happen; they call the church to a bigger vision;

and they're not content with people who hold positions but don't perform. Additionally, coaches are able to see the big picture of a church or an organization.

Because they visualize the big picture, ministers with the coaching style of leadership have the capacity to see how the different facets of the church interrelate, and they approach ministry with a holistic attitude. Coaches are good at helping a church know how to accomplish a goal; assessing who feels called to fulfill certain tasks; and recognizing when and where to begin. The danger is micromanagement. Coaches need to delegate and to provide training for people who have responsibilities in the congregation. People in the pews are frustrated when the minister simply says, "We need to care for the widows." They need to know who can do which tasks and how they can best accomplish them.[2]

Because coach leaders are so passionate about what they want to achieve, one of the fundamental dangers is their tendency to become frustrated and even angry that the congregation is not responding quickly enough. These ministers may spend so much time and energy scolding the congregation for their slowness that they become vulnerable to depression and burnout.

Most of us go into the ministry because we want to make a difference, but we need to balance our desire for change with the recognition that change for all of us is usually painful and slow. We should temper our passion with patience. Otherwise, we can become victims of our own drivenness.

The Counselor

Jackson and Bossé-Smith point out that to understand leadership styles, we need to recognize the starting point for each one. Commanders begin with a view of the future. Coaches start with a vision of the team. Conductors, as we'll see later, start with a vision of the system. On the other hand, counselors see the group as individuals and are concerned about their welfare as persons. Counselor leaders take into strong account each individual's background and whether the people are experiencing personal fulfillment.

Counselors are less concerned about achieving goals as a group and more concerned about relationships. This type of leader is usually well liked by the people with whom she works because folks sense her concern that they grow and find a sense of purpose in life.

Jackson and Bossé-Smith identify two possible downsides to this leadership style. I take some issue with their first concern. The authors claim that since counselors want to be liked, they frequently have difficulty with confrontation. In my experience, counselors with whom I have worked and supervisors of studies like Clinical Pastoral Education have wanted me to grow as a person and as a minister, but they have never been reluctant to confront me in the areas of my life where they believed I needed to change.

Jackson and Bossé-Smith's second critique may be more valid. Because counselors are focused on individuals and on building relationships, they tend not to pay as much attention to organizational issues. Therefore, it's vital for counselor types to build into their organizational system other leaders who are attentive to institutional challenges. Relational pastors need staff ministers or laypeople who focus on the needs of the institution as a whole.

Again, employees or congregants like counselor leaders because they genuinely care. They feel our pain. As a preacher, this leader is effective because he sees the listeners as people with needs, and his sermons usually revolve around real-life issues that we all face. Each of us has experienced some type of difficulty, and in those times we are drawn to a leader and preacher who understands the tall weeds of life.

The fundamental danger counselor leaders face falls within the sweet spot of their strength. Some employees or members of a congregation may constantly have perceived needs. Because their counselor pastor seems to be caring, these members constantly require her time, and her calendar and cell phone become cluttered with urgent requests for "just a few minutes" of her attention. It adds up quickly.[3]

All ministers need to be wise in drawing boundaries and not giving the impression that we are available 24/7. For caring leaders, this is particularly difficult. We are trained to be there for people, but, when we carry our presence to the extreme, we lose energy, become discouraged, and take little time for ourselves and for the tasks of ministry such as preaching.

Counselor-oriented ministers who take time to prepare their sermons can exercise effective leadership from the pulpit. Perhaps the first and one of the finest examples of this type of homiletical leadership was Harry Emerson Fosdick, the outstanding preacher for whom John D. Rockefeller constructed the Riverside Church in New York City. Fosdick labeled his preaching as "client-centered therapy": he began many of his sermons with problems that people faced, and then he sought an answer through a biblical text.

Most counselor preachers are well received because they try to connect the biblical text with issues that most people encounter. For example, we all know what it is to be afraid, discouraged, or lonely. Counselor ministers can exercise effective leadership and gain the trust of listeners because they truly seem to understand "what it is like to be me."

For those of us who are disposed to this type of preaching, the danger is neglecting the prophetic side of the gospel or implicitly assuming that everyone who listens to us has problems. When I did a sabbatical with Dr. Fred Craddock in 1991, he graciously read a textbook that I was writing titled *Preaching from the Inside Out.* After he read my chapter on those who listen to sermons, he looked at me and said, "Everybody you preach to must be sick. You wouldn't know what to do with a healthy listener. All you could do is circle him like a buzzard until he went down." Counselor leaders must be aware of the joyful, contented times in life as well as the ones in which people cry out for help. There's no need to begin every sermon with, "Now what's wrong with you?"

The Conductor

Jackson and Bossé-Smith remind us that no leader fits entirely into one category. While most leaders have a preferred style, they may also find themselves operating from various approaches, often depending on the situation. For example, a leader whose preferred style is to coach may also be a conductor. A conductor likes precision. A conductor expects that anything that is done will be done well.

Conductor leaders love data and the process of gathering all the information pertinent to a situation. They are good at helping a church or organization collect facts in order to predict trends and help shape the vision for the future.

One of the problems for conductors is getting them to stop gathering information so that a decision can be made. Groups often become exhausted with people who think they never have sufficient data and are reluctant to move beyond turning over every rock to see if there's something else to discover. Conductors may have to be told, "We have enough information," even though they believe there's more that the group should know. They sometimes reach the point of sacrificing relationships as they focus on gathering information. These types of leaders need to be encouraged to take risks, although that's antithetical to the way they process situations.[4]

Conductors are, however, useful to any leadership team. We all know the temptation to implement ideas before we've garnered the information we need. Conductors serve as the checks and balances to those who rush to shape a vision and align people behind a plan that is embryonic at best.

The philosopher Franz Kafka talked about a man who jumped on his horse and rode off in all directions at the same time. Every leader needs some of the conductor. Leadership is risky, but it's not reckless. Having sufficient information about the challenges we facing, the resources we possess, and the essential information that we need will keep us from jumping on the horse and riding off in all directions at the same time.

While Jackson and Bossé-Smith do a great service in offering these categories that distinguish leadership styles, I want to discuss four other styles briefly. While each of these has some of the characteristics of Jackson and Bossé-Smith's types, they deserve mention of their own.

Servant Leadership

The modern-day concept of servant leadership was given impetus by Robert Greenleaf, who wrote an essay titled "The Servant as Leader" in 1970.[5] But the concept of servant leadership has been promulgated for many centuries, particularly among religious groups. Those in the Christian faith think of the compelling words of Jesus to his disciples:

> You know that among the Gentiles those whom they recognize as their rulers lord it over them, and their great ones are tyrants over them. But it is not so among you; but whoever wishes to be first among you must be slave of all. For the Son of Man came not to be served but to serve and to give his life a ransom for many. (Mark 10:42-45, NRSV).

While Greenleaf didn't invent the concept of servant leadership, he certainly revived interest in this style. In 1972, Greenleaf expanded his concept to include corporations and other groups. He wrote, "This is my thesis: caring for persons, the more able and the less able serving each other, is the issue upon which a good society is built."[6]

Greenleaf avowed that servant leadership was both a philosophy and a set of leadership practices. In the early 1970s, many of the leadership styles that are prevalent now had not been developed. As Greenleaf observed leadership, the two fundamental options were "autocratic" and "laissez-faire." In other words, a leader could operate from the top down, giving instructions, or simply do little or nothing and let the church or congregation drift into its own shape or fall victim to institutional chaos. Greenleaf preferred the concept of *participative*, and he developed the following traits of a servant leader around that idea:

- *Listening*—being able to hear another's needs and wants.
- *Empathy*—understanding others, which leads to the employee's personal development.
- *Healing*—trying to heal oneself and others, attempting to help people with their problems and conflicts.
- *Awareness*—being aware of one's own self and also aware of others.

• *Persuasion*—not trying to impose ideas but utilizing persuasion.
• *Conceptualization*—thinking of the big picture instead of focusing only on day-to-day problems.
• *Foresight*—being able to foresee likely outcomes of decisions.
• *Stewardship*—holding an institution in trust for the greater good of society.
• *Commitment to growth of people*—including personal, professional, and spiritual growth.
• *Building Community*[7]

Obviously, servant leadership is commendable, particularly for those of us who have committed ourselves to trying to be servants as we follow Christ. The qualities that Greenleaf spelled out are admirable, and if each of us followed them, our world would be a better place.

Servant leadership, however, assumes a high maturity rate on the part of the followers, and sometimes the needed element of challenge and confrontation is missing from a servant leader. Particularly in times of crisis, a leader's desire for growth in herself and in others may need to take the form of tough love. While Jesus certainly called his followers to be servants to others, he also stressed the demands of discipleship. In the beginning of the "journey" section in Luke 9, Jesus is explicit about the cost of discipleship:

> As they [the disciples and Jesus] were going along the road, someone said to him, "I will follow you wherever you go." And Jesus said to him, "Foxes have holes and birds of the air have nests, but the Son of Man has nowhere to lay his head." To another he said, "Follow me." But he said, "Lord, first let me go and bury my father." But Jesus said, "Let the dead bury their own dead, but as for you, go and proclaim the kingdom of God." Another said, "I will follow you, Lord, but first let me say farewell to those at my home." Jesus said to him, "No one who puts his hand to the plow and looks back is fit for the kingdom of God." (Luke 9:57-62, NRSV)

Primal Leadership

Daniel Goleman of Rutgers University emphasized the need for emotional intelligence among leaders. His book, *Primal Leadership: Realizing the Power of Emotional Intelligence*, co-authored with Richard Boyatzis and Annie McKee, became a *New York Times* best-seller. While this book has much to offer, its fundamental principle is this: "The singular notion that sets the most successful CEOs apart from others turned out to be a critical mass of emotional intelligence competencies."[8]

Among many other concepts introduced in this book is the idea of the "resonant leader" and the "dissonant leader." Later, Boyatzis and McKee expanded these concepts in their own book, *Resonant Leadership*. Building largely on the insights of emotional intelligence, Boyatzis and McKee draw a distinction between a leader who helps to create resonance in a group and one whose style of leadership results in dissonance. According to the authors, "EI (Emotional Intelligence) is the key."[9]

EI enables us to monitor ourselves so that we don't react without thinking. Developing self-awareness and self-management enables us to capitalize on our strengths and manage our emotions so we can feel—and create—passionate commitment to goals. Understanding others enables us to motivate individuals and guide groups, teams, and organizational cultures more effectively.[10]

In terms of dissonant leaders who tend to create fear through threat and intimidation, Boyatzis and McKee point out that many of these types didn't start out that way. In a potent warning to all of us who try to lead, the authors remind us, "The constant sacrifices inherent in effective leadership can cause us to lose ourselves and sink into dissonance. . . . Slowly, over many years, we lose touch with our core and what we really care about, and one day we find that we are not ourselves anymore."[11]

Losing our integrity as well as our passion for ministry is a constant threat for ministers. We go into ministry to make a difference, and we inevitably encounter resistance and opposition. This brings us to Adaptive Leadership and the notion of the "sacred heart."

Adaptive Leadership

Adaptive leadership is values-based leadership where a sacred heart is essential to an effective leader. In their book, *Leadership on the Line*, Ronald Heifetz and Martin Linsky describe sacred heart as "the essence of being alive, the innocence, curiosity, and compassion."[12] A sacred heart keeps leaders from becoming numb with the pressures of leadership. As Heifetz and Linsky say, "That's what we learned about the sacred heart—the willingness to feel everything, to hold it all without letting go of your work."[13]

The authors explore their key word, "adaptive," by contrasting it with problems that have a technical solution. For example, if my computer stops working, I take it to a specialist who diagnoses the problem and fixes it in a mechanical way. Most issues that we face, however, are more ambiguous and difficult and thus call for riskier, more adaptive responses. Adaptive leadership requires an understanding of systems theory, since most challenges that we face demand an understanding of the systems that are at work.

Obviously, this only touches the hem of the garment of "adaptive leadership." If you want to see the full range of this excellent philosophy and vision of leadership, I suggest two books in addition to *Leadership on the Line.* Ronald A. Heifetz's *Leadership without Easy Answers* and Heifetz, Linsky, and Alexander Grashow's *The Practice of Adaptive Leadership: Tools and Tactics for Changing Your Organization and the World*, which to me is the most readable of the three, are helpful.[14]

In *The Practice of Adaptive Leadership*, the writers use the phrase, "getting on the balcony," at the end of each chapter. This encourages us to mentally move off the practice field or dance floor to evaluate what is motivating us to play, dance, or work so hard. Being on the balcony gives a leader needed perspective on the busyness of life.

Transformational Leadership

Several years ago, I wrote a book called *Transformational Leadership: Leading with Integrity.*[15] It was an attempt to name and briefly discuss some areas of leadership that I believed were essential. While "transformational leadership" is not a term unique to me, I attempted to discuss aspects of it in an ecclesiastical context. The thesis of the book was that courageous leadership brings about bold, transformational changes in a church.

In my opinion, the day is over for any church to drift from one Sunday to the next without a bold purpose and direction. The stakes are too high; the issues are too important; the gospel itself calls each of us to radical change. This is no time to be playing church! With those things said, I want to discuss three vital aspects of transformational leadership that will inform the rest of this book.

Quality of Leadership

I will always be indebted to Ronald Heifetz for that day he shared the term "sacred heart." It stuck in my mind and has become an important expression of my vocabulary of leadership. Leaders in the church must have a sacred heart—a mixture of compassion, wonder, innocence, and awe. But how do we attain those qualities and then hold them as we face the inevitable difficulties of trying to be the church?

Father Richard Rohr, founder of the Center for Action and Contemplation in New Mexico, writes about our personal transformations in his book on contemplative prayer. Rohr, a Franciscan monk, reminds us that we are part of a much larger story and a much larger self. Our lives become episodic and fragmented when every day is centered on us and how we perceive ourselves to be doing in a particular moment.

Rohr said, "The gift that true contemplatives offer to themselves and society is that they know themselves as part of a much larger story, a much larger self."[16] While this awareness doesn't divest us of all the unnecessary baggage that we carry, which grinds us down or makes us jaded, it does allow us to see ourselves each moment as part of a larger Self (God) and a larger story that began far before we entered history and will probably end far after we leave.

The Risk to Try Something Big

If you are like me, I have an aversion to failure. I would rather pick out the issues on which there is little or no conflict and bravely take my stand. I am a people pleaser, and I want people to like me.

The ministry is filled with people like me. We are nice, kind, and polite, and we love it when someone says, "You're the nicest, best pastor we've ever had."

Without becoming mean and ornery, which most of us ministers unfortunately do just with our immediate families, how do we recover the prophetic dimension of the Bible? How do we speak to the issues that society presents so that the church is not perceived as completely irrelevant? Recently, Pope Francis criticized the priests and nuns of Brazil for not getting out of the church more and speaking in ways that ordinary people could understand. When do you think this Pope will be invited back to Brazil?

But his words are true. A vision for a church is not just about securing finances and making certain that we have adequate facilities for members. It's about engaging the world with the good news of Christ that is often subversive to those who live too lavishly while others go hungry. Leadership is about meeting people where they are, not where we wish they were. It cares for the lonely, the marginalized, the dispossessed, the woman or man whose home is the street.

My own experience is that any church loses its vitality when it's only concerned with herself. If our only outreach is to open the doors on Sunday and hope somebody wanders in, then our prospects of being a church that will make any difference are probably doomed.

A Hope Built on the Presence of Christ

Let's face it. These are not the best days for the church in North America. Maybe in Africa or in Latin or South America, where there seems to be growth and enthusiasm, we can rejoice. But in North America, fewer people are attending church or have interest in denominations or religious activities. This problem seems particularly acute among many young people who feel that churches have lost relevance.

What do we do? We can applaud an interest in spirituality that some folks have. They don't like organized religion, but they don't seem to mind the term "spiritual," as long as they define the word. We can cling to the positive signs in some religious groups and the tremendous growth in mega-churches.

I'm thinking now, however, of many churches that have either plateaued in their growth or have declined. In these churches, the situation is often handled through blame. If only we had a more committed leadership, if only our church was in the growing suburb instead of the inner city, if only . . . the list could go on.

I don't want to see these churches lose the sense of transforming hope that Christ brings us. The church is Christ's body. We fear difficult problems, but we don't face them with our own ingenuity alone. Our particular church may not have the attendance or finances that it once did. It doesn't help to wish for the good old days, because they probably won't return. The challenge is this: with our hope in Jesus Christ, what difference for his sake can we make in this moment that God has given us?

Questions for Reflection

1. Using Jackson and Bossé-Smith's categories of leadership, which one are you most comfortable with and why?

2. Since many church people identify themselves as servant leaders, what components of that style do they sometimes neglect?

3. What is your definition of transformational leadership? What internal things in us and what external factors in the church keep us from exercising bold, risky leadership?

Notes

1. John Jackson and Lorraine Bossé-Smith, *Leveraging Your Leadership Style: Maximizing Your Influence by Discovering the Leader Within* (Nashville: Abingdon Press, 2007) 37–45.

2. Ibid., 47–58.

3. Ibid., 59–67.

4. Ibid., 71–81.

5. See the website for the Robert K. Greenleaf Center for Servant Leadership at greenleaf.org, especially https://greenleaf.org/what-is-servant-leadership/ (accessed 31 March 2014). You can order copies of Greenleaf's two essays from this site.

6. Ibid.

7. Ibid.

8. Daniel Goleman, Richard Boyatzis, and Annie McGee, *Primal Leadership: Realizing the Power of Emotional Intelligence* (Boston: Harvard Business Press, 2002) 82.

9. Richard Boyatzis and Annie McKee, *Resonant Leadership* (Boston: Harvard Business School Press, 2005) 30. Also see chapter 2 above.

10. Boyatkis and McKee, *Resonant Leadership*, 30.

11. Ibid., 66.

12. Ronald A. Heifetz and Marty Linsky, *Leadership on the Line: Staying Alive through the Dangers of Leading* (Boston: Harvard Business Press, 2002) 225. For more on the "sacred heart," see chapter 1 above.

13. Heifetz and Linsky, *Leadership on the Line*, 229.

14. Ronald Heifetz, *Leadership without Easy Answers* (Cambridge MA: Belknap, 1994); Ronald Heifetz, Alexander Grashow, and Marty Linsky, *The Practice of Adaptive Leadership: Tools and Tactics for Changing Your Organization and the World* (Boston: Harvard Business Press, 2009).

15. Charles B. Bugg, *Transformational Leadership: Leading with Integrity* (Macon GA: Smyth & Helwys Publishing, 2010).

16. Richard Rohr, *Everything Belongs: The Gift of Contemplative Prayer* (New York: Crossroad Publishing Company, 2003) 24.

Chapter 5

The Challenge of Church Leadership in a Postmodern World

My mother, dad, and I were baptized in the West Flagler Park Baptist Church in Miami, Florida, in 1955. Later, my younger brother was baptized in the same church. In one sense, that was the best of times for a local church. I remember the church was filled on Sunday mornings and almost filled on Sunday and Wednesday nights, and we were expected to attend Sunday school, church training, and mission groups every Wednesday.

There was little competition for loyalty to the church. In the late 1950s, Elvis Presley appeared on the *Ed Sullivan Show*, and our pastor warned us of the dire consequences of missing the Sunday night service to see this Memphis sensation who swiveled his hips in seductive ways.

The church was the center of my family's world. It was not only the place where we were fed spiritually but also the social center of our lives. While it's tempting to see those times as the good old days, the fact is that they are gone, and perhaps our memories are fonder with the passing of time. I do recall heated business meetings and some caustic remarks directed at our pastor. So, during the 1950s, while sanctuaries were filled, the churches were hardly an ecclesiastical paradise.

Churches in the twenty-first century that once were vibrant places of worship are now half-filled, and the maintenance of older buildings is consuming more and more of often diminishing budgets. In some places of worship, people find themselves in a maintenance mode while any energy for a new vision and fresh ministry approaches is exhausted simply through their efforts to keep what they have going.

While churches face numerous challenges, I want to examine four in particular and consider how we can exercise transformational leadership as we address them.

1. Doing More with Less

If a church's overarching concern is simply to survive, then that congregation is probably already dead. What about our dreams for what God wants us to be? How do we let go of what seemed like the "glory years" in order to live into a new reality with a new purpose and vision? This is the "new normal" for many congregations that have plateaued or declined. They are not able to afford the multiple-clergy staffs that they once enjoyed. Finances have necessitated a hard look at what can be done and what must be left behind. Often, these churches will continue to function with the same vision and a semblance of the same strategies that they have always had. No wonder discouragement sets in. At some point, we have to face reality. That means we have to set goals in light of our resources. We may want to be risky and set goals that stretch us, but the worst approach is to be unrealistic about what we can do and put ourselves in the position of failure and frustration.

When I was fourteen years old, I dreamed about being a major league baseball shortstop. After a game in which I made three errors and struck out twice, the coach pulled me out of the game and put in another shortstop. I decided that major league baseball was not my future. I made an adaptive change.

In our time, we are going to have to make some adaptive changes. Trends show that many people are not giving their money to the church, and this is particularly true of younger generations. People are busy. Their children and grandchildren are playing soccer on Wednesday nights. More affluent people view their weekends as a time to get away. The buildings to which we once devoted so much money and pride are shredding church budgets with their maintenance and upkeep.

How do we respond? This sounds heretical to a Baptist who grew up spending a lot of time coming from and going to the church building, but perhaps one strong worship service on Sunday along with a

Bible study program is sufficient today. If there's a midweek meeting, we need to clarify why we are there. Once we've established our rationale for activities in the church, then we need to communicate our expectations for the roles of church leadership and membership. Let's face it. We have dumbed down discipleship, and we are reaping the consequences.

It is unrealistic for the church to try to be what it used to be without sufficient resources. That path eventually leads to despair. Instead, why not shape our mission statement and outline our strategies to fit the new reality?

This is not defeat. Working with a vision that people can actually accomplish gives the congregation a sense of achievement and hope and may lead the church to expand its ministry as certain realistic goals are met. Most organizations are operating with more short-term goals given the pace of change in our society. Five- and ten-year plans have been abandoned because life in our world is so fluid, and it's difficult to plan that far in advance.

What if a church adopted a mission statement and strategies for each year? This would take some work, but it would allow such details as the budget process and the staffing of teams or committees to coalesce around the ministry the church wants to achieve. This certainly doesn't mean putting the professional staff on one-year contracts. It means better deploying their skills in service of a clear and current church mission. Working on the church mission one year at a time demands commitment from laypeople. I will discuss this further in chapter 6, but if the present is any indication of the future, churches will have to rely more on the commitment and work of all the people. For many congregations, the day is past when they could afford to call more clergy to do most of the work of the church. It may be an opportune time to view all of the members of the church as true ministers and parts of the body of Christ.

2. New Emphasis on Spirituality

In his excellent book *Everything Belongs*, Richard Rohr reminds us of the "alternate reality."[1] Rohr contends that most of us live in the world of the "bottom line." What we can get, achieve, or make for ourselves is our guiding principle for us. Rohr's call to contemplative prayer is a call to open ourselves to a way of living in which the world is a sacred temple, and we learn to embrace the poor, the impoverished, and even those whom we may consider our enemies.

Frankly, people like Rohr, Henri Nouwen, and the Baptist contemplative Glenn Hinson do more to nourish me than the sermons that I preach or even the ones I hear. I relish the kind of spirituality that both challenges and comforts me. Even though I'm a minister, it's sometimes difficult for me to see what I do as little more than ritual.

The problem is that we have a bifurcation between spirituality and religion. Even people who seldom if ever go to church are drawn to speakers and writers who seem to address the void that many of us feel. Younger people who have abandoned going to church services are drawn to religious leaders like the Dalai Lama, who offer a message of balance in an unbalanced world.

What is the answer? How do we bridge the gap between what we traditionally label as religion and the wave of interest in spirituality?

First, we need to recognize that there are significant differences between doing church and being spiritually formed. Whether or not we like to admit it, most churches have the look of a business, and energy and time have to be expended to maintain the institution. As I look at my own ministry, I realize how much of myself as a minister was devoted to maintaining facilities, building new facilities, making sure that expenses didn't exceed income, coordinating events, working with church staff and leaders, and the list could go on. One day, I told my wife that I felt like a firefighter with a squirt gun trying to put out fires.

That doesn't mean I didn't experience significant spiritual highs. As a minister, people invite you into the depths and heights of their lives. You walk with people through the valley of the shadow of death, and you have the opportunity to bless two people as they join their love and lives together. You watch people come to know the Christ. You have the holy privilege to baptize them. You serve the elements at the Lord's Table, and despite all the inadequacies you may feel about it, you have the sacred call to preach the word of God to people.

Would I be a minister if I had it to do over again? The answer is a resounding "yes." But I would keep in mind that the calling to be a minister means that we somehow have to keep near the presence of God in all the messiness that is often a part of the institutional church.

I love Henri Nouwen's words, "Be present to the presence in prayer."[2] I have to remind myself that this wasn't always easy for Nouwen. He struggled at some of the educational institutions where he taught and candidly admitted his lifelong battle to find his own place of peace. If I were to do ministry over again, I would try to be less driven and less ambitious. Those attitudes sometimes resulted in a self-centeredness that caused me to ask, "How am I doing?" rather than "What am I allowing God to do in and through my life?"

As I think about how to bridge the gap between spirituality and the life of the church, a key word is "experience." Transformational leadership moves beyond simply imparting information. Obviously, there are times when the right information helps us solve a problem. The deepest parts of who we are, however, are seldom changed just by the addition of information. Powerful spiritual writers have written imaginatively of a God who can transform our lives and even our world. The process of spiritual formation challenges us to see the world as chock-full of transcendence. Through that process, we don't just describe God; we seek to experience God as the limited horizons of our lives are pushed further and further back.

Perhaps that's what transformational leadership, worship, and proclamation need to do. All of these things are informed by study, but their fundamental purpose is not to recreate the classroom. Instead, their purpose is to create sacred space where people's lives are transformed. The goal of any church should be to help people become examples of transformation in the world God loved and for which God died.

3. The Reality of Plurality and Inclusion

For a long time, one of the fundamental tenets of church growth was homogeneity. The principle was that "like elicits like." At a lunch some years ago, a creative, well-known writer and speaker on trends and characteristics of churches that were experiencing numerical growth said to a group of us that few churches grow unless they are homogeneous. His contention was that if you want upper-class people to come to your church, you begin with a nucleus of people in the same socioeconomic group. If you want a congregation of people who are theologically conservative, you call a conservative pastor who attracts people who mirror the desired theology of the church.

While it's difficult to argue with "like attracts like," I raised the issue of ecclesiology. What about the foundational doctrine of the church? While most if not all of Jesus' first disciples came from the peasant group and were largely illiterate, as the church grew, it reached the educated, the affluent, and many who were socially prominent. Jesus' invitation is to all people regardless of their differences. The genius of the Christian faith is that it embraces diversity, rejects uniformity, and finds unity in faith in Jesus Christ as Lord.

I understood what the Christian speaker and futurist was saying about homogeneity. Any church certainly grows faster if its people dress fashionably and embrace the same sort of doctrines with smiles on their faces. After all, it doesn't help the image of the "Church of the Upper Crust" to have a beat-up truck sitting in the middle of shiny BMWs.

But is finding the quickest way to church growth really the issue, or is it trying to get the Jew, the Gentile, and the Samaritan to find common ground? Our world is becoming more diverse each day. Consider the United States. The Caucasian population is now a minority. The growth of the Hispanic, African-American, and other ethnic populations are making churches face certain questions: How do we reach out to each other? Does 11 a.m. on Sunday morning remain the most segregated hour in the week? If it does, what can we do to change that?

This is only a slice of the diversity that we face in our times. Navigating doctrinal disputes, addressing social issues such as the place of women in some faith communities, understanding the concerns of the LGBT community, and choosing liturgical styles and types of music used in worship services are also part of the diverse religious world. Shall I go on? Obviously, there are not enough pages to begin to cover the disputes that many denominations and congregations are facing today.

How does transformational leadership respond to this diversity and to the heated emotions that these issues often generate? First, some of these concerns need to be faced directly, and that entails risks for a leader. A minister has to follow her interpretations of Scripture, do her own study and analysis of the situation, and then choose what she believes is the right thing to do. We may want to lessen the stakes in our discussion of these challenges, but the fact is that some people think that the crux of their faith is threatened if the church does not decide what they want.

I wish there was a way to make everybody happy with the church, but my own experience proves that this is an illusion. People have minds, they have emotions, and they have voices. They don't always discuss every issue in a calm, rational way. A leader needs to keep his wits about him and not increase the level of ire by trying to outshout someone else. We seek light—not a torched church house.

At the same time, the leader needs to keep the focus of the church on the mission of following Christ and serving others. Timing is a key component in the life of the church. As strongly as I may feel about an issue, I want to introduce it to the congregation in a respectful way. I need to ask the question, "What is the best strategy for getting this accomplished?" Trying to barrel through resistance without considering why it is present and how I should deal with it is not courage. It is often foolishness.

4. Social Issues

Social issues tie directly to a world that is exploding with a variety of people from various cultural contexts. Our growth is putting more and more strain on natural resources. In a world where countries such as China, India, Brazil, and others are rivaling the United States and many European countries in their need for oil and petroleum products, we face a crisis that can't be ignored.

Later, I will talk about how transformational leadership influences our approach to this and other cultural and social issues. Having grown up in a strong evangelical background, I saw that the primary emphasis was on changing individuals. Our ministers used the word "evangelism" when they called for change. That referred to the church's task of bringing people who were not Christians into a saving relationship with the God revealed in Jesus Christ. While we were admonished to live moral lives, the primary payoff of our salvation experience was that we would go to heaven and escape hell when we died.

A lot of energy was generated by this worldview. What we lacked, however, was any sense of the social implications of the gospel—unless it referred to avoiding alcohol, not having sex outside of or before marriage, and not dancing. I probably never would have thought about any of the evils of dancing if visiting evangelists hadn't painted such vivid pictures in their sermons. Smoking cigarettes, on the other hand, seemed more acceptable since all of us had to walk through the secondhand smoke of deacons when they were supposed to be welcoming us but seemed more intent on getting the last puff before the call to worship.

The church in the twenty-first century is different. While many churches still stress evangelism or the call to faith, some of those same churches and others are addressing the social, cultural, and economic issues of our day. For these churches, the gospel is incomplete with just the conversion of the individual. Instead, they believe that systems within society need to be changed so that groups of people don't needlessly suffer or feel marginalized from an inclusive view of the church.

There are many social, cultural, and economic issues confronting the church today, but I have picked four. I want to try to offer some ways that transformational leadership can have a positive impact in each area.

Disparity of Wealth and the Issue of Poverty

Although it's not always recognized, the gap between those who have enough or more than enough and those who barely subsist is drastically increasing. This is not only a moral issue but also a social and spiritual one.

Consider America and the collapse of the middle class as the rich get richer and the poor get poorer. Recently, many workers in the fast food industry went on strike, seeking a livable minimum wage. Their actions were met by resistance from the company owners, who felt that higher wages would cut into their profit margins.

Consider many other places in our world. Some of these areas are tinder boxes already exploding or threatening to explode. While there are multiple causes such as religious or sectarian differences, riots in the streets are also fueled by people who can't find jobs and resent those who have more than enough while they have virtually nothing. Poverty feeds discontent, and we shouldn't be surprised by the anger of parents who can barely feed their families.

How does the church respond to such an overwhelming problem? Since much of it involves political change, we need to support those who are trying to do what is morally right and responsible, and we need to be careful not to support a political agenda that is simply in our nation's best interest. We transform a situation by looking at it as best we can through the eyes of Jesus and by remembering his constant call to care for the poor, the needy, and those who don't hold the reins of earthly power.

Transformational leaders also need to have the courage to speak truth to power. By the world's standards, most of us who read these words are wealthy. Like many of you, our family has a nice home, two cars, a retirement plan, and some savings. At times, I wish I had more, but that's precisely the problem.

Many of us have more than enough. Some people have way too much, considering the poverty in the world. When do we start to give away our stuff or become a part of groups that are making a difference in the world? Transformational leadership helps us understand that the response to the grace of God is generosity.

The Environment

In the ongoing debate about how to interpret the creation stories in Genesis 1 and 2, one vital element is often forgotten. Stewardship for creation is the responsibility of humankind. God said, "Let us make humankind in our image, according to our likeness; and let them have dominion over the fish of the sea, and over the birds of the air, and over the cattle and over all the wild animals of the earth, and over every creeping thing that creeps upon the earth" (Gen 1:26).

As archaic as these words may sound to modern ears, they are a clear call to you and me to care for the world that God has created. But what is happening to this earth that we inhabit? Tragically, there are many signs that, instead of being stewards, we are actually destroying what God has created.

In *The Christian Century*, Eileen Flanagan wrote an alarming article titled "Temperature Rising," in which she spoke about the consequences of rising temperatures on the continent of Africa:

> Increasing temperatures produce the changes that can have dire consequences for farmers. Warmer winters mean that pests may not die off between growing seasons; scorching heat in the spring and summer means that rain may evaporate before it's absorbed into the ground. Warmer air also holds moisture longer, so rain becomes less frequent but heavier when it finally does come.[3]

What is happening in Africa is also happening throughout our world. Excessive use of fossil fuels and carbon dioxide emissions are melting polar ice caps and creating rising sea levels. Is this a natural phenomenon that will pass in time? Some have economic interests that cause them to take this position, but the vast majority of climate scientists believe that we are killing the world that God created and called good.

Transformational leadership will have to run the risk of angering certain economic interests, even some of the people in our churches. The bottom line is that destroying our ecosystem is a spiritual and moral issue. To say nothing is to be compliant with forces that selfishly destroy our planet, and maybe, worst of all, it is to fail to be stewards of a creation that God has entrusted to us.

Violence and Guns

Those of us who live in the United States are witnessing an outcropping of violence not seen in any other civilized country in the world. The proliferation of guns, the lack of strict background checks, and the continuing stream of violent video games, television shows, and movies feed the tragic sense that killing another human being is a part of the rhythm of life.

Added to this is the fact that mentally ill people gain access to guns, and we have disasters like the shootings in Newtown, Connecticut; Aurora, Colorado; Tucson, Arizona; and close calls at places like an elementary school in Decatur, Georgia. We have a dangerous situation when our children and innocent people are slaughtered with assault rifles. Recently, a young baseball player from Australia was shot in the back while he was jogging in Oklahoma, and the three teenagers who were arrested confessed that they shot him because they were bored. The right to bear arms is a guaranteed constitutional right in the United States, but what is happening goes far beyond someone owning a gun for hunting purposes or a small handgun for self-protection.

How does a transformational leader respond? First, we need to emphasize the sanctity of a human life. In the name of freedom to bear arms, we have opened the floodgates to the easy availability of handguns in addition to automatic rifles, complete with magazines and a number of bullets that result in human slaughter. Police forces are outnumbered by people who possess far more firepower than they do.

The issue is whether the protection of gun rights is more important than the people who are being killed. Julia Lene, an Australian writer, noted the contrast between the homicide rates in Australia and in the United States. Following a mass shooting in 1996, the Australian government embarked on a stringent licensing and gun-regulation process. Lene pointed out that there are still about a million handguns in Australia, but they are carefully licensed, and no one would think about carrying a gun in public.[4] Consequently, the homicide rate in Australia is 0.13 per 100,000 people. According to GunPolicy.org, the tragic difference is 3.6 per 100,000 persons in the United States.

Transformational leaders will take a big risk on this issue; the gun lobby in our country has proven its strength, and our culture often glorifies violence. But those statistics represent people who are created by God, and we can hardly continue to live in a nation where even the local newscasts begin with somebody's being shot and killed. This is not a partisan political issue. Ask parents of the children killed in the Newtown tragedy. This is a moral and spiritual issue that demands a prophetic word from the pulpit.

Human Sexuality

I don't remember much, if any, positive talk about sexuality when I was a teenager growing up in church. We could have used some in our youth group. After all, we were teenagers bursting with hormonal changes, and it would have been nice to know that we were normal.

Basically, we were told to grow up, get married, have children, and be faithful to our spouses. Maybe God was looking out for me because I have been able to realize my dream. Diane and I have been married for forty-six years; we have two children, and beyond the serious illness of our son, we have endured the minor bumps and bruises that come from any close relationship. I have experienced incredible joy in the road that I have chosen.

With more people experiencing divorce, however, the challenge to churches is how to minister to these people whose lives have been radically altered. How do we minister to children who don't understand why Mommy and Daddy don't live together? Churches also have to develop safe places such as Sunday school classes and Bible study groups through which people who have experienced the trauma of divorce can find their way again into the stream of church life.

Some have suggested the idea of "covenant" as a metaphor for marriage. In the Bible, a covenant is a sacred commitment of two parties to each other. Each party has responsibilities to the other, but the covenant is seen as an agreement under the aegis of God.

One of the most challenging issues for many congregations today is whether gay and lesbian persons have a right to domestic partnerships or marriages, if allowed in their states. I have watched good friendships end over disagreement on this issue. Some churches affirm gay-lesbian relationships and offer themselves as "welcoming and affirming" communities. For other churches, the thought of a same-sex marriage is anathema. While the Bible doesn't speak extensively on this issue, a few verses are used to fortify the position against gays and lesbians. Of course, some biblical scholars see these verses applying to abuses of any kind of sexual behavior, including heterosexuality.

Those of us in the free-church tradition strongly affirm the "autonomy of the local church." That means that no hierarchical group dictates doctrines or positions on social issues to a congregation.

That's why, for example, Baptist churches are different from each other. Despite the best intentions of a minister, no one person or small group has the right to dictate the course of a church.

There is a difference between leading people and pushing people. Leadership respects the views of others regardless of whether they are mine. Pushing people is a form of "clerical bullying" that usually results in increased resistance.

A wise friend of mine always talks about "seeing the Christ in the other person." This doesn't mean that we always agree with that person's behavior, but we never stop seeing one other as persons created in God's image.

For many people, especially those in younger generations, acceptance of gays and lesbians is a given. This doesn't apply to all young people, but I have talked with many who have grown up accepting sexual differences. For those of us who are older, the struggle to accept LGBT lifestyles has been more intense. Throughout most of my life, even the American Psychiatric Association viewed homosexuality as a mental illness. Of course, that has changed.

I suppose that certain streams have fed my acceptance of gay and lesbian persons. First, I have come to know some of them as friends and have found them to be remarkably kind and caring. I'm certain that not every gay person is gracious, but many of them have experienced exclusion and rejection, and, in a way, this has "tenderized" them.

Second, I have spent much of my life assuming that one's sexual preference was a personal choice. I thought it was like walking into Baskin-Robbins and picking chocolate or vanilla. I'm now convinced that sexual preference is not a choice. Our nature and nurture both play a part in determining who we grow up to be.

Third, I am trying to follow my friend's advice to see "the Christ in the other person." Same-gender attraction is alien to my way of thinking and acting, and yet there are people who are attracted to same-gender partners. My task as a minister/leader is to try to understand the differences in people and to love them without putting labels on them.

I've shared where I stand, but a transformational leader wants to help people understand certain things. First, how we stand on the gay-lesbian issue should not be the litmus test for being a good Christian. Second, we don't want to make this a generational issue of younger people versus older people. Talk to people of all ages, and you'll find different positions. Third, as a minister approaches a church on this issue, she needs to be aware of where her congregation stands on this matter and be sensitive to "timing." It does nobody any good if we say the right thing at the wrong time. We can always begin with, "Let's see the Christ in the other person."

Questions for Reflection

1. What do you think your church will look like in ten years, and how will that affect the way you will do ministry?

2. What would you say to a person who says, "I'm spiritual but not religious and not connected to any church"?

3. What is your response to the social issues the author listed? Is it possible to disagree on some of these issues and still remain friends and committed to the idea that "Jesus is Lord"?

Notes

1. Richard Rohr, *Everything Belongs: The Gift of Contemplative Prayer* (New York: Crossroad Publishing Company, 2003).

2. Henri Nouwen with Michael J. Christensen and Rebecca J. Laird, *Discernment: Reading the Signs of Daily Life* (New York: Harper One, 2013) 145.

3. Eileen Flanagan, "Temperature Rising," *The Christian Century*, 12 August 2013, p. 22, http://www.christiancentury.org/article/2013-08/temperature-rising (accessed 1 April 2014).

4. Julia Lene, "Slaying Focuses Australia on U.S. Gun Culture," *Herald Leader* (Lexington KY), 27 August 2013, p. 9.

Chapter 6

Can Clergy and Laypeople Work Together?

Many observers of churches believe that there is increasing conflict between the clergy and what we call laypeople. This doesn't mean that every church is embroiled in conflict. Some congregations exist largely in harmony and have found effective ways to deal with any conflict that surfaces.

But these churches seem to be more the exception than the rule. While some of the conflicted churches may not have reached the point where the conflict is public and known throughout the congregation, an undercurrent of dissatisfaction sabotages the ministry of the church. Recently, a person in a church where I was a guest pastor described a spirit of malaise in the congregation, which he attributed largely to the ineffectiveness of the pastor.

What causes this kind of conflict? Besides the fact that there may be people in the church who are chronically dissatisfied, we may have to ask if our ordained ministers are prepared for the realities of the church. Many ministers have had the benefit of excellent academic training in a seminary or divinity school, but they make the transition into the church with no sufficient training in some of the practical areas of ministry or in time management or conflict resolution. Periodic sabbaticals for ministers where they can work on needed areas of growth would pay great dividends both for the ministers and the churches they serve.

Churches in Decline

An older minister friend of mine told me how grateful he was that he did his ministry when the church was more at the center of people's lives. He is right to notice the downward trend of many churches in North America and Europe. While churches in Africa, Latin America, and South America seem to be experiencing some growth, many churches, particularly in the United States, are experiencing an alarming decline in both attendance and financial support.

This often leads to a blame game. Older people in the church remember when "Dr. Jones" was pastor, the pews were filled with people, buildings were erected, and programs were replete with people eager to be a part of the church. They feel that the current decline must be the preacher's fault. If they just had a pastor who knew how to connect the Bible to people's needs, the pews would be packed. Meanwhile, the clergy bemoan the lack of strong lay leadership. This back and forth blame game does nothing to effect positive difference.

Clergy and Laypeople in Opposition

In one excellent church where I served as the pastor, the deacons were known as the "board." While the vast majority of the deacons saw their roles as supportive of the ministerial staff, a few viewed their calling as being part of the legislative branch. While the ministerial staff functioned as the executive branch, a few of the deacons perceived that their role was to serve as a check and balance on the functioning of the ministerial staff.

Obviously, every good clergy person is open to the suggestions and even the negative criticism of laypeople. When this becomes the primary means of operating, however, an over/against mentality sets in.

In this particular church, I made a strong effort to create a body of deacons that was committed to servant ministry. We even created a deacon-staff team so that, in a manageable setting, we could discuss issues of vital concern and share ways to do ministry more effectively.

I wish that my suggestion had resulted in an overwhelming success. While our church moved toward the idea of family ministry and the deacons assumed a larger share of servant leadership, the idea of a "board of directors" was firmly implanted in the minds of some of our leadership. Our deacons' meetings were interesting. For a time we would discuss the needs of church members, and then, at some point, we were back to the staff and how we could do our ministries better. While most remarks were made in a good spirit, they were usually too vague and unfocused to be of much help.

Somehow, despite our differences, all of us in the church need to understand that we are on the same team and are committed to the mission of serving Christ.

No Shared Vision

Some churches have no stated vision for their ministry and thus nothing to coalesce the variety of expectations for the church. A vision statement does more than call the congregation to a sense of common purpose. It also limits people's expectations so that the church isn't trying to do everything, getting frustrated in the process and winding up blaming each other because members are all functioning with their individual expectations of what the church should be.

The church with a clear vision is better able to deal with the source of most contention between laypeople and clergy. Think of all the different expectations that people have of their minister and the priority of those expectations. Usually, a congregation wants an effective preacher. But what does an effective preacher sound like? Is she a good storyteller whose sermons are loaded with interesting illustrations, or is she an expository preacher whose fundamental task is to teach the biblical text? What about her delivery?

Some people in a church are looking for a pastor. Will he be there when I'm in the hospital? Does he visit elderly members who are at home or in nursing homes?

What about the pastor's administrative/leadership skills? Do committees or teams in the church know what they're supposed to do? Is there a sense of the "big picture," or is the ministry of the church episodic and fragmented?

To compound the problem, some people in the church expect their minister to do all of these things well in addition to taking care of himself and spending sufficient time with his family. When I was a seminary student, a well-meaning professor said that we should spend one hour of preparation for every minute we were in the pulpit. Interestingly, this professor had never been the pastor of a church.

How nice it would be to have an hour to prepare for every minute that I preach! But with the other tasks of ministry, this is totally unrealistic. Also, it's unrealistic to expect any minister to score "10's" in every phase of ministry. This leads me to some ways in which clergy and laypeople can become ministers together and further the vital work of the church.

The Ministry of the Baptized

Norma Cook Everist and Craig L. Nessan use the powerful phrase, "ministry of the baptized," in their book, *Transforming Leadership.*[1] For many of us in the free-church tradition, baptism is the public statement of a personal transformation after a person decides to follow Jesus Christ as personal Savior and Lord. Often, those of us who view baptism in this way may use the phrase, "age of accountability." This simply means that a person should be able to understand the rudiments of what it is to be a follower of Christ before making a profession of faith and then being baptized.

Other faith traditions view baptism as one's becoming a part of the larger community of faith called the church. This may happen when an individual is an infant, but often it is followed later in life by catechetical studies and confirmation.

Obviously, for different people, these are both legitimate interpretations of baptism. But what is the primary purpose of baptism?

Henri Nouwen focuses strongly on the baptism of Jesus himself. He is moved by the words of the Heavenly Father to his Son at his baptism: "You are my beloved Son in whom I am well pleased." Nouwen is struck by the fact that this happens at the beginning of Jesus' ministry. In other words, Jesus has preached no sermons, performed no miracles, and spoken no parables, but the Father blesses him with unconditional love. For Nouwen and many of us, this is incredibly good news. Neither Jesus nor any of us has to earn God's love. Our baptism is a strong affirmation that we are loved not for what we do but for who we are.[2]

A second aspect of Jesus' baptism is that it marks the beginning of his public ministry. Our own baptism is the starting point of our ministries. The church is a body of baptized believers. But the way we express that belief is not by finding a seat and watching others serve God and people. Baptism is a call to vocation and to service. We discover the gifts that we can use to serve God, and the church becomes the "ministry of the baptized."

Sometimes people ask, "Don't we pay our professional staff to do the ministry?" Obviously, the paid staff members of the church have more time to focus on ministerial tasks. Those of us who are clergy have had hands laid on us as we've been set apart to pursue our calling. Some of us have had the opportunity to attend seminary or divinity school, where we've received special training to be ministers.

But sharing the ministry with the congregation does not mean the ordained ministers are trying to shirk their tasks. We should set the example in taking our roles seriously and doing our best to fulfill them. And a great part of a clergy person's calling is to affirm people's gifts and help equip them to serve. In this way, we become the "ministry of the baptized."

The Life of Prayer

Many of us think of our Christian faith as activity done in the name of God. We become busy about many things and often feel depleted by our constant doing. Our active bent leads us to redouble our efforts, usually resulting in more fatigue and less focus.

It can help to start a new emphasis on spiritual formation and prayer together as a church. Prayer makes us realize that we are dependent on God. What if clergy and laypeople came together in a sense of dependence on the Transcendent One? Prayer brings us together because, no matter who we are, we are God's. We are not ultimately accountable to ourselves or to each other, but we are accountable to the God who receives us in God's gracious love.

I recognize that I have spent far too much of my life trying to achieve and to gain the approval of others. For the most part—though not always—I have succeeded. Yet living life for approval is like eating popcorn at the movie theater. Do you stop with one or two bites? Try it! I've gone to the movies with my wife, had the best intentions to take two or three pieces of popcorn, and you know the rest of the story. It's impossible to stop.

"In contemplative prayer," writes Richard Rohr, "we move into a different realm. It is not the arena of merit, of reward and punishment; it is the realm of pure grace and freedom. It is such an utterly different world from the ground up that most religion drags along the reward/punishment system since it can understand no other."[3]

What if the sense of sheer grace pervaded a church so that all people saw themselves as servants of Christ? What if we could eliminate the insatiable appetite for approval and applause and were no longer consumed by a win/lose mentality? What if our own egos were submerged, and, whether clergy or laypeople, we were all ministers committed to serving the Christ?

The Life of Service

Between the writing of the Gospels and our time, something terribly sad and perverse has happened to the call to faith. Jesus called people to follow him, learn from Him, and serve the needs of others in his name. Jesus never intended his disciples to join an organization or even a church. The call to follow was a dynamic call, and the early band of believers could best be described as a "movement."

Over the course of time, the church took on the offices and look of an organization. At the same time, thoughtful followers of Jesus kept calling the church back to its fundamental identity of a living organism, not just a sterile organization. As editor Dorothy C. Bass states in the preface to *Practicing Our Faith*,

> . . . [M]any thoughtful Christians . . . yearn for a richer and deeper understanding of what it means to live as Christians in a time when basic patterns of human relationship are changing all around us. We want to know what Christian faith has to do with our work, with friendship and marriage, with the way we raise our children, with problems and practical life, with how we spend our money.[4]

When churches become embroiled in conflict, it's often because both laypeople and clergy lose sight of the fact that we are ministers called to serve God and the world that God created. The church is not just an organization called to prop up and perpetuate the structure. We may have different titles or designations in the church, but our fundamental calling is to serve rather than to be served.

Recently, I preached at a church in Louisville, Kentucky, and an elderly man whom I later learned was ninety-two years old came forward during the invitation to join the church. His daughter and son-in-law helped him walk to the pastor at the front of the church.

When he was welcomed publically by the congregation, the pastor greeted him, and in a loud, strong voice, the man said, "I have joined this church to serve."

After the worship service was over, I met this man who had come to serve. On his suit coat I saw a Purple Heart given to him in World War II. I suspect service was in this man's blood. As a pastor, I've heard people say a lot of things when they come forward during the invitation. Some want to be baptized. Some want to join the church. Some want their children to be in the church's programs, and it would be better if the whole family joined. What I don't remember is anyone ever coming during the invitation to say, "I want to serve."

I don't know how many ways this man whose daughter and son-in-law helped him to the front will be able to serve, but I suspect that he will find his place and be a real asset to that ministry.

Can laypeople and clergy work together? The answer is a resounding "yes" if we see ourselves as fellow ministers who are called to serve the Christ and the world that he loved and for which he died.

A Community of Worship

Worship is both a public and private act. Through prayer, Bible reading, contemplation, and reflection, we spend time alone with the Alone. While we offer our petitions to God, intercede for those who are in need, and express adoration and gratitude, we fundamentally acknowledge the worth of God and the central place we pray for God to play in our thoughts and actions. In our private times of worship, we seek to center our lives on the Holy One and pray for forgiveness, direction, and guidance.

When we speak about worship, it's important for us to remember those private times when we try to align our wills with the will of God. Private moments of worship help steady us in a world filled with events and unexpected occurrences that can make us anxious and wondering if life has any real purpose. Those who worship well privately can worship well communally.

The act of communal worship is a major part of a Christian's life. How do transformational leaders approach these times when we gather to sing songs, pray, preach, share in the sacraments or ordinances, give offerings, and, most important, be invited to follow Jesus Christ into his work of loving and calling people to follow him?

Transformational leaders need to keep the focus on realizing the worth of God. Regardless of whether a person is an ordained clergy or a layperson, the commitment to a high view of worship and its possibility to transform people's lives is essential. The tasks in the worship service may differ, but the primary purpose of realizing God's worth for our lives is the same.

Since I've been a pastor and preaching minister for most of my life, I realize how important laypeople have been to my own ministry. Words of encouragement, expressions of prayerful support, and the kindness of paying attention have been incredible gifts to me as a person and a pastor. As a preaching minister, I have come to realize that most of us feel some inadequacy in trying to fashion words that, Sunday by Sunday, speak to the lives of people. I preached my first sermon when I was fifteen years old. That's fifty-five years ago. Someone said to me, "You must be used to it by now." I hope that as long as I'm able to preach, I never get used to it.

God decides to put God's treasure in our earthen vessels, and that means that as ministers, we never stop being human. We need to strike a balance between anxiety that freezes us and humility that keeps us aware of our dependence on God. Communal worship brings the community of faith together around a shared commitment to the worth of God. As long as we keep our focus on this God whom we worship, our conflicts and problems won't take us off our main focus.

In times when I may feel spiritually dry, I try to remind myself that the worship of God doesn't depend on how scintillating the sermon may be. What we do in the worship service is an offering to God. While we want to offer our best, the amazing thing is that God is able to take our offering and do with it what we can't imagine. After all, it is treasure in earthen vessels.

Across the Great Divide

In my opinion, one of the most stimulating authors of our time is Parker Palmer. In his book, *A Hidden Wholeness,* he has a chapter titled "Across the Great Divide." He talks about the need for trust in God and in each other in a world shredded with differences and distrust. Additionally, Palmer stresses the importance of each of us living an integral life, staying true to the principles that guide us. As Palmer states, "No one wants to suffer the penalties that come from living divided. But there can be no greater suffering than living a lifelong lie."[5]

How do we learn to live a life of personal integration? Palmer commends the place of solitude and prayer, but, more than that, he emphasizes the role of community, what he calls "a circle of trust."[6] Obviously, this is more than accidental community. It's built on trust of each other, an intentional community that has to be desired and pursued.

What fractures community? We may have different opinions, but I would say that it's a lack of trust. Clergy and laypeople interact with each other's lives, and often we come to know each other at a deep level. Unless we operate with unrealistic expectations, we don't expect perfection that belongs only to God. But we do expect openness, vulnerability, and respect for each other.

I still recall a sermon that I preached as a pastor when I was in my thirties. I was angry with the congregation because, in the middle of the summer, the church had dropped in attendance and giving. I saw myself as the prophet Amos, which is presumptuous enough. The people who were in the service that Sunday hadn't gone to the beach or to Disney World. They'd probably put their offerings in the collection plates, never expecting a sermon that would peel the bark off their trees. (By the way, when I started to teach preaching, I told this story and warned the students that it was never a good idea to carry rage into the pulpit.)

I'm sure there were some who were upset with my caricature of Amos, but most of the parishioners were extremely gracious. Some people thought that I had been working too hard and wanted to take up a collection to send me on vacation. In retrospect, maybe I should have played the overworked pastor who needed a month lounging somewhere in the Caribbean.

The fact is that I wasn't that tired. I thought I was angry that people weren't responding the way I felt they should. Then an insightful deacon got at the heart of what was happening. Stopping by the office on Monday afternoon following the "shootout at First Baptist," he kindly said, "I didn't hear madness: I heard profound sadness. You were sad because you couldn't make everyone do what you wanted them to do." As so often happens, we ministers convert our sadness into "madness," and then we have the audacity to believe that we are prophetic.

I apologized to the church because my sadness caused me to speak in a way that showed disrespect. Instead, I believe that my asking for forgiveness was a way of helping to seal our trust in each other.

We try to build a circle of trust, and we call that the church. Maybe a few people expect perfection in the rigid, graceless way that some folks have. We will never satisfy those people, and they may not be satisfied by much of anything. As laypeople and clergy, however, we continue to try to please God and then are grateful that God is so eager to forgive.

Questions for Reflection

1. How would you describe the relationship between laypeople and clergy in your church?

2. Do you think that the pressures and challenges many churches face today contribute to the notion that more congregations seem to have a higher level of conflict?

3. How can we help churches understand that all who follow the Christ are ministers and not just members of the church?

Notes

1. Norma Cook Everist and Craig L. Nessan, *Transforming Leadership: New Vision for a Church on Mission* (Minneapolis: Fortress Press, 2008) 200.

2. Henri Nouwen, *The Only Necessary Thing: Living a Prayerful Life*, comp. and ed. Wendy Wilson Greer (New York: Crossroad Publishing Company, 1999) 67.

3. Richard Rohr, *Everything Belongs: The Gift of Contemplative Prayer* (New York: Crossroad Publishing Company, 1999) 99.

4. Dorothy C. Bass, ed. *Practicing Our Faith: A Way of Life for a Searching People* (San Francisco: Jossey-Bass, 2010) x.

5. Parker Palmer, *A Hidden Wholeness: The Journey Toward an Undivided Life* (San Fransisco: Jossey-Bass, 2004) 20.

6. Ibid., 22.

Chapter 7

The Power of a Renewed Vision for the Church

"What is your church's vision?" Ask some church members that question, and you may get the answer, "To survive." I don't want to be too hard on these churches. Some of them are living on the thin diet of memories from a time when their churches had financial resources and a leadership base that gave them visionary guidance.

But things change. I can think of churches in the inner city whose members across the years have been drawn to churches in their nearby suburbs that offer a more convenient, full-service ministry. Some people have remained loyal to the home church, but these folks are growing older and don't have the energy or the money to bring back the good old days.

I can think of churches that have experienced devastating conflict, and droves of people have scattered to other places of worship. Perhaps it was a theological conflict, maybe an interpersonal disagreement. Whatever the issue, those who believe they won the battle are now rattling around a worship center far too big for their numbers. The lack of people screams to guests, "What happened in this church to cause so few people to participate?"

These situations are unfortunate, but there are probably few churches that haven't undergone some degree of disagreement or even turmoil in their histories. What keeps a congregation focused and directed during the evolution of its ministry? At the risk of oversimplification, I believe that one of the strongest forces for cohesion is the congregation's clear sense of vision.

Peter L. Steinke is probably most well known for his statement that a pastor or transformational leader should be a non-anxious presence in the context in which she works and ministers. Steinke observes, "Congregations that lack a focus are like a sailor on a lake without a destination with no port in mind; the sailor will not know how to adjust the sails to guide its course. The sailboat will drift or meander. Congregations not focused on the mission (destination) meander or float aimlessly too."[1]

Steinke draws attention to a minister friend of his, Sterling Nash, who was approaching his sixtieth birthday. Each year, Nash would facilitate a leader's retreat in his church using Peter Drucker's five questions for corporate self-assessment.

1. What is our mission?
2. Who is our sustainer?
3. What does the customer value?
4. What are the results?
5. What is our plan?

One year, Nash decided to have the group members answer the questions, except, as they responded, they were to imagine themselves as the following people:

- A fifteen-year-old
- A migrant worker
- A single parent
- A new convert
- A parent with teenage children
- A fifty-nine-year-old minister not sure if he's on empty.[2]

Steinke's observations remind us that a vision statement should be closely connected to the context in which it serves. While a mission statement may be broad, such as "Love Jesus and Others," a *vision statement* should focus more on the specific needs of a particular group or congregation. I suggest that a vision statement may be modified each year to address the changing needs of the church. The vision may affect the way a church apportions part of its yearly budget, and it will make each year's priorities clear to the church members and staff.

In their excellent book, *Leadership 2.0,* Travis Bradberry and Jean Greaves offer some unique and important suggestions about visioning.

The authors speak about vision under the broader rubric of strategy. Using the Apple company as their model, they state that it takes vision, acumen, planning, and ultimately courage to make change happen.[3] In other words, creating an effective vision is not enough. It takes acumen (knowledge of your congregation and the world in which it functions), planning (how to implement the vision), and courage and risk to make changes.

While each of those things is vitally important to a vibrant church, the idea of strategy begins with a clear, focused vision. Again, the vision needs to be related to the specific challenges of the church. What hinders many churches is that there is either no vision or a vision so broad that the people can't get their heads, hearts, and hands around it. "Winning the world for Jesus" is a noble calling, but it probably leaves most congregations without enough specificity to visualize the task and to make plans to accomplish such an imposing mission.

Bradberry and Greaves present several guidelines for an organization as it develops a vision.

Create the Vision

"You want your vision to change the way people see their work," the writers state. "It should motivate all to act without self-interest in the pursuit of a superordinate goal."[4]

Bradberry and Greaves say that, while it is good for churches to post their vision statements around the building, doing so often has little or nothing to do with decisions the church makes or the way the congregation operates. Much more than a slogan or catchphrase for the church, "the purpose of a vision is to create a direction for the organization that people can believe in."[5]

This is hard work and requires the input of as much of the congregation as possible. Many churches have lost a sense of direction and operate from one crisis or decision to the next. In some congregations, people have become confused and tired because they have no sense of the big picture of the church. That's the value of having both a vision statement and a plan to implement it. Instead of being reactive to every situation, the church can become proactive because the people know what the vision is.

Often, you can tell whether a church has a sense of direction by observing committee meetings. If the meetings are conducted in a way that seems to have no purpose, and if the meetings take too much time because the conversation is monopolized by a few people who want to talk about everything in general and nothing specific, those are telltale signs that there's no guiding vision.

Trying to get a congregation to congeal around a shared vision is certainly a risky task for leaders. First, churches and other groups have a way of running on their own inertia. If worship services are held, Bible study groups are meeting, and the congregation is sending money to support mission work, then the idea is, "If it's not broken, why fix it?" But we all know the danger that arises when our routine ways of operating are threatened by any kind of significant change.

Second, trying to stay relevant with a strong vision and making plans to implement it is demanding work. Everybody in the church has other things to do, and the transformational leader needs to be open and honest that seeking God's direction requires prayer, conversation, and commitment. One way to begin this process is to start with something that the congregation can easily do so that the church will start with a victory.

For example, if a church decides to reach out to the community, the people may begin by creating a clothes closet. Assuming that there are people in fairly close proximity to the church who need additional clothes for their children and themselves, this closet should be well organized, with hours of operation clearly posted and with church members to help facilitate access to the clothes for those who need it. It won't work if church members simply bring clothing they don't want and pile it in a room with no order. Whatever task is chosen, the idea is to help the congregation see that it can do something well and gain both the confidence to expand the vision and the means to achieve that vision.

Don't Confuse Values with Vision

Bradberry and Greaves write that values include ideas like teamwork and excellence.[6] Strong values are essential for any organization. For example, the lack of teamwork among a church staff or leaders of a congregation can quickly sabotage the best intentions for ministry.

Problems among a staff or with the leaders of the church are palpable, so that even strangers walking into the room can feel the tension. From my experience as pastor, I realize that the temptation is for us to think that we can work out our problems internally. A wiser course, however, may be hiring a trained coach or consultant to get a good, outside perspective on the problem. Most teamwork problems don't resolve naturally. They continue to fester, making the work environment toxic. Or, perhaps worse, a trigger causes the situation to explode, and everyone is wounded.

While strong values are essential to the working of a church, these values are not a vision. A vision is more of a statement of what we want to accomplish. Values like strong teamwork and a desire for excellence help a congregation achieve that bold vision.

Give Them Something to Talk About

According to Bradberry and Greaves, a vision "must balance being realistic and feasible with being audacious enough to drive people and get them to let go of their routines. It should be brief enough to be easily communicated, yet detailed enough that people know it well."[7]

The vision for the church should be something that can be memorized and communicated easily throughout the congregation. Each member should be able to learn and tell it to each other. For example, Bill Hybels, pastor of the Willow Creek Community Church in suburban Chicago, began his ministry to reach "Unchurched Harry and Unchurched Mary," fictional characters who were described as the church's target audience.[8]

With this simple vision statement, Willow Creek Church has grown explosively over the years. A lot of planning and work have gone into the realization of this vision. But guiding every aspect of what Willow Creek does is its passion to attract people who are unchurched.

Not every church will be drawn to the Willow Creek model. George Barna speaks of a church in the northwest part of the United States that has the following vision statement: "To provide the greater metropolitan area with a church geared to the needs and life-style of baby boomers who are nominal Christians, offering a ministry that is sensitive in personality and characterized by a loving, forgiving, and accepting environment."[9] This vision statement is outdated. Today, we may talk about reaching the Gen Xers or Millennials.

A vision statement will not say all that a church should do, but it does give focus to the way a church shapes its ministry. How do we fashion our worship services? How do we provide education in a way that utilizes the interactive technology that the current generation is accustomed to using? Questions like these can help a church be inclusive of all ages.

Establish a Sense of Freedom

Once the group owns the vision, what is the role of the leader? Is she a micromanager who follows people around to make certain that everything is done exactly the way she wants? Does a transformational leader become authoritarian in his approach, intimidating and threatening people into doing everything precisely his way? Bradberry and Greaves are clear that neither of these two approaches is helpful.

Instead, the leader needs to trust people and honor their freedom to use their gifts to achieve the vision.[10] Both micromanagement and authoritarian styles are symptoms of the leader's insecurity and unwillingness to trust others to do the work. When a leader takes this approach, the people begin to feel that this is not their vision and not their work. After a time, they lose interest and feel less invested in what they're doing.

A vision is not *my* vision; it needs to be *our* vision. That means that each person in the organization is trusted to use his or her gifts and initiative to accomplish the task. Obviously, this assumes that a plan has been developed so that each person is clear about his or her role. Members of a symphony orchestra may all know how to play their instruments, but the conductor needs to lead them in the same musical number. It won't work if the orchestra's vision is to play, but everybody plays a different song. Likewise, the eleven players on offense on a football team are destined to lose if each one decides to run his own play. When a play is called by the coach or by the quarterback, it becomes the vision for that moment, and each payer has a role to execute.

Freedom is not permission to act any way we want and create chaos and confusion in the organization. Freedom is discovering/

discerning our God-given gifts and using them with other members of the body of Christ to further the reign of God.

Test Your Vision

Finally, Bradberry and Greaves encourage a leader or group to test the new vision by asking six important questions.

1. Is the vision easy for other people to see?
2. Does the vision stimulate their interest?
3. Does the vision get people moving spontaneously?
4. Is the vision realistic?
5. Is the vision so clear that people can spread the word?
6. Would everyone continue to pursue the vision even in the leader's absence?[11]

While most of these six criteria are self-explanatory, I want to offer a few words of explanation that echo some of Bradberry's and Greaves's observations.

First, when we talk about a vision being easy for others to see, we are examining the ability to articulate the vision clearly. A vision may be born in the leader's mind or in a group process. Usually, there are a cascade of ideas and thoughts. Sometimes we have a variety of ideas swirling through our minds, but we need to arrive at one focus that we understand and can clearly communicate to others.

Second, a vision should give people both direction *and* a sense of energy and excitement to pursue the vision. That energy begins with the leader. If he is not excited about what is ahead, the people in the church will likely take a similar attitude. Nothing kills a vision more quickly than for a congregation to pick up an attitude from the leader that they're making a change not because they're excited about it but because they have to do something.

Third, trying to reach a vision together should not feel like a forced march. Neither should leaders have to push people to do something in which their heads and hearts are not invested. If there's indifference or even resistance to achieving the vision, then the vision needs to be rethought and, perhaps, redone. People should feel self-motivated, taking the initiative to use their gifts and skills in order to actualize the vision. When a vision engages people's spontaneity and they are eager to work, that is the sign of a vibrant vision.

Fourth, while a vision needs to be challenging to people, we don't want to make it so overwhelming that people can't achieve it. That results in frustration and a sense of failure. In fashioning a vision, a leader should take into account both what needs to be done and the resources that are available. In churches where there are few resources in terms of people or finances, it's better to set an achievable goal and allow people to have a small victory. This builds confidence, and, in time, it allows larger goals to be set.

Fifth, visions can be spread in a variety of ways. We can post them in strategic places around the church building so that folks are constantly reminded of our focus. The best way for a vision to spread, however, is by word of mouth. This means crafting a succinct and clear vision statement that people can remember. The vision needs to be articulated with attention to its oral quality. A vision statement needs to be amenable to memorizing and sharing. To facilitate this sharing, the vision also needs to make people feel excited about what it calls the congregation to become. Without an almost palpable sense of direction within the church, the vision may be easy to memorize, but there will be little energy to share it with others.

The sixth and final test that Bradberry and Greaves offer is whether people would continue pursuing the vision statement without the leader. A vision should not be about the leader or tethered so closely to what she wants that enthusiasm for the vision is dependent on her presence and persuasion. This is why any vision needs to be supported or owned by as many people as possible.

As a former pastor, I remember the possessiveness that I had about a good idea. In a sense, it was my "baby," and I didn't want others to tell me that my baby wasn't the best and most beautiful. In presenting this baby or vision to the church, I had to be careful not to become overly defensive or try to push something on people for which they didn't share my commitment or energy. Usually, what emerged from this process of give and take was something that resembled my baby but certainly had features that meant it was "our" baby.

A real test of leadership is whether a church can continue to function at a high level even after a pastor or strong staff person has left the scene. Has the congregation learned how to create a vision, plan, deal with conflict, have a sense of mission, and do the many other things that healthy churches do, even if their leader leaves or changes?

Begin Where You Are

An organization or church needs to begin the visioning process by asking honestly, "Where are we now?" Some churches should start with a vision that will help them survive the changes they are facing and gain a sense of confidence. These churches face a new reality. While some of the members long for the glory days of the congregation, the people will have to grieve what has been lost and move to a different future where they can serve Christ in different ways.

Other churches have more people and resources. These congregations need to discern what the passion and gifts of the people are. The temptation is to try to do everything, but there will always be things that a particular church doesn't do well, and that can cause frustration. Learning to let go of what doesn't fit our passions is as much a part of visioning as deciding what constitutes our mission and vision in the first place.

Questions for Reflection

1. What is the vision of your church? If you don't have one, pray about it and write a vision statement that you believe fits your congregation.

2. Why do you think it might be important for a congregation to revisit its vision statement once a year?

3. If you have a vision statement, what steps do you need to take to make certain that it is "owned" by the congregation?

Notes

1. Peter L. Steinke, *Congregational Leadership in Anxious Times: Being Calm and Courageous No Matter What* (Herndon VA: Alban Institute, 2006) 71–72.

2. Ibid., 72.

3. Travis Bradberry and Jean Greaves, *Leadership 2.0* (San Diego: Talent Smart, 2012) 24.

4. Ibid., 23–24.

5. Ibid., 24.

6. Ibid., 25.

7. Ibid., 26.

8. Ibid.

9. George Barna, *The Power of Vision: Discover and Apply God's Plan for Your Life and Ministry* (Ventura CA: Regal Books, 1992) 23.

10. *Leadership 2.0*, 34.

11. Ibid., 27–28.

Chapter 8

The Ultimate Question: Was Jesus a Transformational Leader?

Throughout this book, the call has been for you and me to become more transformational leaders. Defining transformational leadership is difficult because it intersects other leadership styles and has much in common with forms like adaptive and servant leadership. But a few unique qualities stand out. Whatever primary styles we adopt in areas of our ministry such as preaching, worship, or pastoral care, most of us learn from others and then develop our own ways to lead. While we should keep growing and developing our ways of ministry, we have to operate within the boundaries of our personalities and the gifts that God has given to us.

In some ways, this chapter is the most difficult to write because the last thing I want is to reduce Jesus simply to a model of leadership. My faith sees Jesus as infinitely more than a model of any form of leadership. When I preach, I'm calling others and myself to a radical reorientation of our lives. I grew up in a church where words like "Lord," "Savior," and "Christ" were applied to Jesus. While these terms were not always well defined, those of us in the congregation knew what they meant: that God in Jesus Christ was calling us to center our lives on this God who had taken on human form for our sakes.

In my own preaching today, I don't take for granted that any of us in the church house, including myself, understand all the theological terms that sound alien to a world where these words are seldom used in Monday–Saturday discourse. In fact, in preaching and teaching, I've found it more effective to describe rather than to define. After all, this is what Jesus did as a Jewish teacher. The Apostle Paul was more into logical arguments that followed the example of

Greco-Roman teachers, but Jesus told stories. "The Parable of the Prodigal Son" or, as some have labeled it, "The Parable of the Waiting Father" is perhaps the best known of Jesus' stories, and it provides a verbal picture that stays glued to our minds.

Because of my faith commitment to this love of God most fully revealed in Jesus the Christ and made known through the working of the Holy Spirit, I have an aversion to looking at Jesus as simply a "transformational leader." He is so much more. With that caveat, however, and in the spirit of late-night television personality David Letterman, I want to give my top ten list of Jesus' qualities that reflect the desire to be a bold, visionary leader.

#10: Jesus' Call to Conversion: A Radical Reorientation of Life

Jesus never intended to start a new religion. Born a Jew, he remained loyal to his Jewish roots while at the same time trying to expand the meaning and application of the Torah or Jewish law. But then, at the end of the first century and early second century CE, Jesus' resurrection formally spurred a new religious faith that we call Christianity, and his followers became more than another Jewish sect.

The Gospels, written after the death of Jesus and seeing his ministry through the lens of his being raised from the dead, present his preaching and teaching as a call to fundamental change. The Greek word, *metanoia*, was used to describe the radical reorientation of life to which Jesus called his listeners.

For example, John's Gospel, probably written about 90 CE, portrays a conversation between Jesus and the respected rabbi, ruler, and member of the Sanhedrin, Nicodemus, in which Jesus tells him that he must be born "from above." This is a supernatural experience that Jesus compares to the wind. Jesus says that we don't know where the wind comes from or where it is going, but we hear the wind and experience its transforming change in our lives.

Following this conversation between Nicodemus and Jesus, the Gospel of John records a soliloquy in which Jesus states, "For God so loved the world that he gave his only Son, so that everyone who believes in him may not perish but may have eternal life" (3:16, NRSV).

New Testament scholars may disagree about whether these are the actual words of Jesus or reflect the faith of the Johannine community (the community related to the Apostle John). Regardless, this is only one instance in the canon of Scripture where Jesus was viewed as more than just an itinerant Jewish teacher; he was recognized as the "anointed one" who had come to call people to follow the kingdom or reign of God.

#9: A Large, Compelling Vision

Transformational leaders function with a large, compelling vision for their organization. In Jesus' case, it wasn't an organization but a movement.

An example of a bold vision is found in Matthew's Gospel in what is called the "Sermon on the Mount." In chapters 5–7, Matthew pulls together the heart of Jesus' ethical and spiritual teachings. Without rejecting the Jewish Torah or the laws by which Jesus has been nurtured, this young rabbi deepens the heart of Jewish teaching. Not only should one not commit murder, but also Jesus takes it a step further: one should also not possess an angry, vengeful spirit. This is merely one example of where Jesus reminds his followers to pay attention to attitudes as well as actions.

In the midst of his teaching on the mount, Jesus gives the disciples a bold directive for life: "But strive first for the kingdom of God and his righteousness, and all these things will be given to you as well" (Matt 6:33, NRSV). While Jesus teaches more in the Gospels about what this statement means, here he gives his disciples an audacious vision that he hopes will guide their lives and the lives of his followers throughout the history of the movement.

#8: The Desire to Create a Team

In all four of the Gospels, Jesus calls together a team, which we refer to as the disciples. A good leader doesn't operate in isolation. She needs the support, advice, and even the criticism of others in order to make the best decisions.

You and I may question whether Jesus received these benefits from his band of brothers. All of the Gospels, but especially Mark, portray the disciples as slow to understand, concerned for their welfare and safety, and even willing to desert or betray Jesus. Even so, Jesus never disbanded his "church." These twelve men followed him as he traveled from place to place. Apparently, Jesus had the ability to see "goodness" even in the "badness" of the disciples.

One of the most impressive practices of Jesus' faith in his followers comes at the end of Matthew's Gospel. The eleven disciples, now that Judas has betrayed Jesus, go to the mountain in Galilee. Jesus meets them after his resurrection. On this Galilean mountain, Jesus entrusts the eleven with what we call the Great Commission: "Go and make disciples of all nations . . ." (16:19). Despite his disciples' failings, Jesus never stopped expecting big things from his team of disciples.

#7: Appeal to the Group's Intrinsic Motives

Recently, I watched a television clip about DeMarcus Cousins, a former basketball player for the University of Kentucky. Cousins played one year for Kentucky before he turned professional. He had recently signed a professional contract for $62 million. I don't know whether the money was spread over five years, but that still is a lot more than I ever made as a minister. In fact, it wasn't until I started teaching that I even had tenure. As a pastor, I remember that, theoretically, I could be terminated with thirty days' notice.

Cousins has what we call "extrinsic motivation." As long as he plays well, he's paid well. A large salary provides a great deal of motivation in sports and business careers. The better a company performs, the more a CEO makes in salary or bonuses.

Intrinsic motivation, however, is when the appeal is made to our compassion or love for God and other people. While some preachers have pronounced a gospel of health and wealth, this seems to be diametrically opposed to Jesus' teaching, which emphasizes the simplicity of life and concern for others.

For example, in Luke 10 when Jesus commissions the seventy to go in pairs into the world, he specifically says, "Carry no purse, no bag, no sandals . . ." (v. 4a, NRSV). Recently, I went to another city to preach a "Fall Festival of Faith." I thought about this passage of Scripture as I lumbered into the airport with a stuffed luggage bag, a suit bag, and a briefcase. I didn't have a purse, but I did have my wallet!

Motivation for service is also intrinsic. One of the great Hebrew Bible Scriptures bears the Hebrew word, *Shema*. In Matthew 10, when a Jewish lawyer asks Jesus what is the greatest commandment, Jesus reaches into both the lawyer's and his own heritage and repeats the *Shema*: "'You shall love the Lord your God with all your heart, and with all your soul, and with all your mind.' This is the first and greatest commandment. And a second is like it: 'You shall love your neighbor as yourself'" (Matt 22:36b-39).

Jesus had intrinsic motivation and instilled it in his followers. Today's transformational church leaders will be spurred by this kind of motivation.

#6: Ability to Self-differentiate

In his excellent book, *How Your Church Family Works*, Peter L. Steinke employs systems' theory to understand how congregations function. Along with other advocates of systems' theory such as Murray Bowen, Steinke employs the term "self-differentiated" to describe healthful functioning, particularly when the system has become riddled with anxiety.[1]

Obviously, nothing in the New Testament is directly about self-differentiation, but the concept is certainly seen in the way Jesus functions. As Steinke points out, the two main needs of life—separateness and closeness—are opposites. The problem arises when anxiety in a situation pushes us into one extreme or another. For example, our anxiety may cause us to withdraw or to become isolated from others. On the other hand, we may err on the side of closeness so that our emotional system is built on pleasing others. We become willing to do anything in order to be accepted and to be liked. Systems' theorists refer to this as "fusing," a condition in which our own identity is lost as we seek to be accepted and loved.

Jesus was a healthy, self-differentiated person. He knew how to experience closeness. He wept over the death of his friend, Lazarus, and perhaps wept at the inability of his enemies to see that his power to change was benevolent and not malevolent. Jesus wept in the final hours of his life as he looked over the city of Jerusalem and realized that he was not going to be seen as their Messiah. Before Jesus preached to the crowds in the desert and multiplied the loaves and fish, he saw the crowd as "sheep without a shepherd." This is a caring metaphor.

Yet Jesus maintained his distance and didn't surrender his identity in times of anxiety, disappointment, and even treachery. Though he loved people, he didn't become "fused" with them and risk twisting his appropriate love into a need for their approval. Jesus kept his focus and sense of mission, and, even in the most traumatic times, he didn't surrender either to isolation or to a closeness that smothered his ministry.

#5: Flexibility: The Willingness to Change

For many of us, change is difficult. Whether it's changing ideas or ways of doing things, it usually feels more comfortable to stay with what we know and what we believe. Change upsets our "homeostasis" or balance. For a time in the midst of change, we feel off-balance, and there is a sense of loss or grief at what we've let go of as an individual or a church.

There are two main cautions with regard to change. First, change simply for change's sake is not good! We need an overarching reason for the change, and this should be explained carefully to an organization. I'm familiar with an organization that is undergoing change in some of its structure, and the leaders are facilitating the change well. First, the head of the organization is spending an extraordinary amount of time meeting and talking with supporters. This builds trust. Second, the interim period before she arrived as head of the organization was effectively used to let people know that structural changes were imperative. Many of the effective people have been retained, and, with retirements and resignations, this has given the leader an opportunity to help shape the organization in a somewhat different way and to hire highly motivated and skilled people for the open positions.

Was Jesus this type of transformational leader? No, not in the sense that he ever terminated one of his disciples, although he may have been tempted to on occasion. But Jesus certainly exhibited the ability to be flexible and to change course when circumstances dictated the need. Each of the Synoptic Gospels records Jesus' return to speak in his hometown synagogue of Nazareth. Luke's account in chapter 4 indicates that Jesus was doing well in his sermon. His listeners were receiving him graciously. But then, in their minds, the preacher went too far. He began to talk about God's love for non-Jewish people in the Old Testament, and this fit one of Luke's favorite themes: that God loves the Gentiles as well as the Jews, and a person does not have to become a Jew before he becomes a Christian. These words infuriated Jesus' hometown hearers, and they tried to kill him. Jesus, however, walked through their midst and continued his ministry at Capernaum.

Think about this story. Surely Jesus was hurt by the rejection at Nazareth, but it didn't freeze his ministry. Second, Jesus called the people to change, but he didn't take responsibility for their not changing. We can't force people to change their ways or ideas. All we can do is try to speak what we believe to be the truth, but change belongs to God. Finally, Jesus stayed faithful to his message even though it wasn't always positively received. The Gospel of Luke and its companion volume, Acts, is about God's love for everybody, and Jesus was faithful to that message.

#4: The Willingness to Challenge Life as It Is

A transformational leader always walks a fine line. Some things in life need to be challenged because they are unfair and unjust. None of us, however, can live on a constant diet of challenge. We need words of comfort that guide us through the difficult moments of life.

Jesus seems to strike that balance. He was not just the "apocalyptic prophet," as some have portrayed him, preaching that "the end is near" and focusing only on making things right. He certainly had a tender spirit that led him to touch the untouchables, heal the seriously ill, and change people's lives so that hope replaced hopelessness.

Yet Jesus also challenged the systems that bound people and the political and religious rulers who tended to restrict the joy of life rather than expand it. Jesus' death was caused not so much by his teachings or his mighty works but rather by his threat to the stability of the Roman Empire and its rule in Palestine.

The Roman leaders seemed reluctant to kill Jesus, but his presence was causing disruption among some of the Jewish leadership. What the Romans could not tolerate was severe disruption to their *Pax Romana*, the peace that the empire had imposed on its inhabitants. In reading the biblical accounts of Jesus' death, we need to be careful not to hold the Jewish people responsible for Jesus' death more than others; the Roman Empire could not tolerate what they interpreted as revolution and treason.

A transformational leader must be willing to run the risk of challenging the unjust ways of life. While this may not lead to death as it did for Jesus, it may lead to some level of persecution and personal distress.

#3: Ability to Face Rejection and Failure

Was Jesus a success? It depends on how we define success. He was faithful to his mission. Jesus had a charisma that drew crowds to listen to his message, although he didn't gain a sizeable number of followers during his lifetime. Following his death and resurrection, the Jesus movement took on new energy and vibrancy. The letters of the New Testament reflect growth particularly among Gentile converts.

While those of us who have staked our lives on Jesus as Lord read his ministry and teachings as guidelines, we can hardly make the case that Jesus was a raving success every place he went. Jesus faced rejection, scorn, and misunderstanding countless times in his life. Even Jesus' means of death, dying on a cross (wood from tree), was seen as cursed in the Hebrew Scriptures (Deut 21:22-23).

If our notion of success is always being well liked, having all of our suggestions unanimously received, and never knowing the pain of rejection, then we have to eliminate Jesus as a success. But if we talk of leadership as being true to our values, making a difference in the lives of some people, and running severe risks to try to accomplish our goals, then Jesus was a transforming leader.

This is a good reminder to those of us in ministry. As a seminary student, I went to a part-time country church with the thought that 100 percent of the people would like my preaching, my leadership, and my pastoral skills. About a month into what turned out to be a five-year pastorate, a woman said to me at the door after the morning service, "Our last pastor used to preach against sin!"

I assumed that, in her mind, I wasn't bold enough to tackle sin. Later, I asked her what sins the former pastor was against. You probably guessed them: "Drinking, smoking, and dancing." Interestingly, she did mention that the former pastor would drive his car well above the speed limit on those hilly, country roads.

As far as I knew, nobody in the church had a problem with alcohol or dancing. We did have one man who smoked a pipe. So I kept preaching on themes like compassion, forgiveness, and hope, which I thought the church needed more. But this experience at the outset of my ministry was a good reminder that we can't please all the people all the time, and we probably won't please some of the people any of the time. Rejection and failure are simply part of leadership.

#2: Willingness to Sacrifice in Order to Achieve a Purpose

Suppose someone asked, "What is the purpose of life?" I'd like to think that I would answer with a big, bold statement about serving Christ and making a positive difference in the world. The plain fact is that on some days, my purpose would be to make it through the day, pay my bills, or just get by. Once in a while I have breakthrough moments when I see that I have been created for a greater purpose and want to do something risky and big for the sake of God.

What is it like to live life for the sake of some great purpose? In the four Gospels in the New Testament, we don't find a day-by-day account of every moment of Jesus' life. Instead, there are four accounts fashioned after Jesus had died, and these accounts have both similarities and variances. Interestingly, the church resisted the efforts of some leaders like Tatian and Marcion in the second century to collapse the four Gospels into one. The church preferred to live on the memories and perspectives of the four communities because it gave the followers of Jesus a fuller, richer account of the life of their Lord.

There are gaps in the life of Jesus. After he was born in such a miraculous way, what did he do as a child? He must have studied the Jewish law since he impressed the temple scholars at the age of twelve when his parents took him to Jerusalem. What about Jesus' adolescence and early adulthood? The canonical Gospels are silent about a formative part in all of our lives.

What we do know is that at about thirty years of age, Jesus emerged on the scene to be baptized by his cousin, John. After resisting the temptations in the wilderness, Jesus began to call together his disciples. As Matthew records, Jesus then started his public ministry: "Jesus went throughout Galilee, teaching in their synagogues and proclaiming the good news of the kingdom and curing every disease and every sickness among the people" (4:23, NRSV).

The Gospels are replete with Jesus' teaching and preaching, his healings and his revolutionary call to the rule of God. Eventually, what he did or how he did it led him to the ignoble death on a cross outside Jerusalem. Looking back, the writers of the New Testament saw Jesus' death as a sacrifice for people's sins and failures and his resurrection as a sign of hope.

To Christians throughout the generations, Jesus literally gave himself for the big purpose of forgiveness and the promise of "eternal life." For people like the Apostle Paul, it wasn't just religious or political enemies that crucified Jesus; it was also the fatal flaw of our resistance to the goodness God. In effect, Jesus came to show us God and to bring us into relationship with that Merciful Other, and he was willing to sacrifice in order to convey that message.

#1: Overwhelming Desire to Give Life and Hope to People

A transformational leader wants to bring positive change and hope into the lives of other people. Sometimes, people argue about whether individuals like Adolf Hitler were leaders. Some people possess personal magnetism, have a charisma that draws people to their causes, and have a consuming passion that, as in Hitler's case, can mobilize an entire country along with allied nations. Despite the tragic consequences of Hitler's influence, some people look at what he was able to do and think this qualifies him as a leader.

Transformational leaders, however, look at the purpose of leadership and ask this question: Is my leadership for the benefit of humankind, or does it cause a division that is detrimental to the good of the majority of people? In other words, do I seek to bring life and hope to others?

While everybody did not welcome Jesus, he made a strong attempt to express the profound ways that he could change people's lives. In John's Gospel, we find a series of "I am" statements applied to Jesus. For his Jewish hearers, this would have been an echo of God's name in Hebrew Scriptures, "Yahweh" or "I am."

Among other designations, Jesus is the "I am" who is the "light of the world" or the "good shepherd." The Johannine community wanted to portray Jesus as the divine one who brought light, hope, safety, and eternal life to all who were struggling to find these things.

Again, Jesus is viewed in the Gospels as far more than just an exemplary leader. Yet, in carrying out his mission, he embodies and espouses those qualities from which we can all learn. In our world today, each of us is looking and listening for the voice that can bring hope amid despair and a word of life where we experience so much destruction and death. Some of us will be leaders who follow in the footsteps of Jesus, guiding people to transform their lives into something bigger, better, and more meaningful in the kingdom of God.

Questions for Reflection

1. What qualities of Jesus as a leader do we need to incorporate into our churches today?

2. In a world obsessed with success and numbers, how do we convince people in our churches that Jesus was a transformational leader?

3. Do you think "transformational leader" is the right term to apply to Jesus? If not, how would you describe the way he led?

Note

1. Peter L. Steinke, *How Your Church Family Works: Understanding Congregations as Emotional Systems* (Herndon VA: Alban Institute) 29.

Other available titles from SMYTH & HELWYS

#Connect

Reaching Youth Across the Digital Divide

Brian Foreman

Reaching our youth across the digital divide is a struggle for parents, ministers, and other adults who work with Generation Z—today's teenagers. *#Connect* leads readers into the technological landscape, encourages conversations with teenagers, and reminds us all to be the presence of Christ in every facet of our lives. *978-1-57312-693-9 120 pages/pb* ***$13.00***

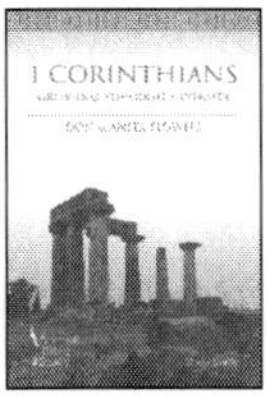

1 Corinthians (Smyth & Helwys Annual Bible Study series)

Growing through Diversity

Don & Anita Flowers

Don and Anita Flowers present this comprehensive study of 1 Corinthians, filled with scholarly insight and dealing with such varied topics as marriage and sexuality, spiritual gifts and love, and diversity and unity. The authors examine Paul's relationship with the church in Corinth as well as the culture of that city to give context to topics that can seem far removed from Christian life today. *Teaching Guide 978-1-57312-701-1 122 pages/pb* ***$14.00***

Study Guide 978-1-57312-705-9 52 pages/pb ***$6.00***

Beyond the American Dream

Millard Fuller

In 1968, Millard finished the story of his journey from pauper to millionaire to home builder. His wife, Linda, occasionally would ask him about getting it published, but Millard would reply, "Not now. I'm too busy." This is that story. *978-1-57312-563-5 272 pages/pb* ***$20.00***

Blissful Affliction

The Ministry and Misery of Writing

Judson Edwards

Edwards draws from more than forty years of writing experience to explore why we use the written word to change lives and how to improve the writing craft. *978-1-57312-594-9 144 pages/pb* ***$15.00***

To order call 1-800-747-3016 or visit www.helwys.com

Choosing Gratitude

Learning to Love the Life You Have

James A. Autry

Autry reminds us that gratitude is a choice, a spiritual—not social—process. He suggests that if we cultivate gratitude as a way of being, we may not change the world and its ills, but we can change our response to the world. If we fill our lives with moments of gratitude, we will indeed love the life we have. *978-1-57312-614-4 144 pages/pb* ***$15.00***

Choosing Gratitude 365 Days a Year

Your Daily Guide to Grateful Living

James A. Autry and Sally J. Pederson

Filled with quotes, poems, and the inspired voices of both Pederson and Autry, in a society consumed by fears of not having "enough"—money, possessions, security, and so on—this book suggests that if we cultivate gratitude as a way of being, we may not change the world and its ills, but we can change our response to the world. *978-1-57312-689-2 210 pages/pb* ***$18.00***

Contextualizing the Gospel

A Homiletic Commentary on 1 Corinthians

Brian L. Harbour

Harbour examines every part of Paul's letter, providing a rich resource for those who want to struggle with the difficult texts as well as the simple texts, who want to know how God's word—all of it—intersects with their lives today. *978-1-57312-589-5 240 pages/pb* ***$19.00***

Dance Lessons

Moving to the Beat of God's Heart

Jeanie Miley

Miley shares her joys and struggles a she learns to "dance" with the Spirit of the Living God. *978-1-57312-622-9 240 pages/pb* ***$19.00***

A Divine Duet

Ministry and Motherhood

Alicia Davis Porterfield, ed.

Each essay in this inspiring collection is as different as the mother-minister who wrote it, from theologians to chaplains, inner-city ministers to rural-poverty ministers, youth pastors to preachers, mothers who have adopted, birthed, and done both.

978-1-57312-676-2 146 pages/pb ***$16.00***

To order call 1-800-747-3016 or visit www.helwys.com

The Enoch Factor

The Sacred Art of Knowing God

Steve McSwain

The Enoch Factor is a persuasive argument for a more enlightened religious dialogue in America, one that affirms the goals of all religions—guiding followers in self-awareness, finding serenity and happiness, and discovering what the author describes as "the sacred art of knowing God." *978-1-57312-556-7 256 pages/pb* ***$21.00***

Ethics as if Jesus Mattered

Essays in Honor of Glen H. Stassen

Rick Axtell, Michelle Tooley, Michael L. Westmoreland-White, eds.

Ethics as if Jesus Mattered will introduce Stassen's work to a new generation, advance dialogue and debate in Christian ethics, and inspire more faithful discipleship just as it honors one whom the contributors consider a mentor. *978-1-57312-695-3 234 pages/pb* ***$18.00***

Healing Our Hurts

Coping with Difficult Emotions

Daniel Bagby

In *Healing Our Hurts*, Daniel Bagby identifies and explains all the dynamics at play in these complex emotions. Offering practical biblical insights to these feelings, he interprets faith-based responses to separate overly religious piety from true, natural human emotion. This book helps us learn how to deal with life's difficult emotions in a redemptive and responsible way. *978-1-57312-613-7 144 pages/pb* ***$15.00***

Help! I Teach Youth Sunday School

Brian Foreman, Bo Prosser, and David Woody

Real-life stories are mingled with information on Youth and their culture, common myths about Sunday School, a new way of preparing the Sunday school lesson, creative teaching ideas, ways to think about growing a class, and how to reach out for new members and reach in to old members. *1-57312-427-3 128 pages/pb* ***$14.0***

Hope for the Thinking Christian

Seeking a Path of Faith through Everyday Life

Stephen Reese

Readers who want to confront their faith more directly, to think it through and be open to God in an individual, authentic, spiritual encounter will find a resonant voice in Stephen Reese.

978-1-57312-553-6 160 pages/pb ***$16.00***

To order call 1-800-747-3016 or visit www.helwys.com

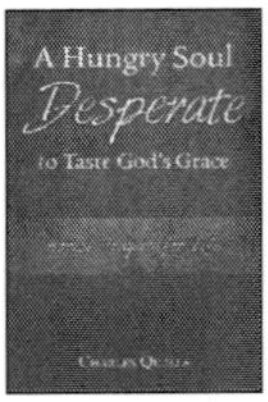

A Hungry Soul Desperate to Taste God's Grace

Honest Prayers for Life

Charles Qualls

Part of how we *see* God is determined by how we *listen* to God. There is so much noise and movement in the world that competes with images of God. This noise would drown out God's beckoning voice and distract us. Charles Qualls's newest book offers readers prayers for that journey toward the meaning and mystery of God. *978-1-57312-648-9 152 pages/pb* ***$14.00***

James M. Dunn and Soul Freedom

Aaron Douglas Weaver

James Milton Dunn, over the last fifty years, has been the most aggressive Baptist proponent for religious liberty in the United States. Soul freedom—voluntary, uncoerced faith and an unfettered individual conscience before God—is the basis of his understanding of church-state separation and the historic Baptist basis of religious liberty. *978-1-57312-590-1 224 pages/pb* ***$18.00***

The Jesus Tribe

Following Christ in the Land of the Empire

Ronnie McBrayer

The Jesus Tribe fleshes out the implications, possibilities, contradictions, and complexities of what it means to live within the Jesus Tribe and in the shadow of the American Empire.

978-1-57312-592-5 208 pages/pb ***$17.00***

Judaism

A Brief Guide to Faith and Practice

Sharon Pace

Sharon Pace's newest book is a sensitive and comprehensive introduction to Judaism. What is it like to be born into the Jewish community? How does belief in the One God and a universal morality shape the way in which Jews see the world? How does one find meaning in life and the courage to endure suffering? How does one mark joy and forge community ties? *978-1-57312-644-1 144 pages/pb* ***$16.00***

Lessons from the Cloth 2

501 More One Minute Motivators for Leaders

Bo Prosser and Charles Qualls

As the force that drives organizations to accomplishment, leadership is at a crucial point in churches, corporations, families, and almost every arena of life. In this follow-up to their first volume, Prosser and Qualls will inspire you to keep growing in your leadership career.

978-1-57312-665-6 152 pages/pb ***$11.00***

Let Me More of Their Beauty See

Reading Familiar Verses in Context

Diane G. Chen

Let Me More of Their Beauty See offers eight examples of how attention to the historical and literary settings can safeguard against taking a text out of context, bring out its transforming power in greater dimension, and help us apply Scripture appropriately in our daily lives.

978-1-57312-564-2 160 pages/pb ***$17.00***

Looking Around for God

The Strangely Reverent Observations of an Unconventional Christian

James A. Autry

Looking Around for God, Autry's tenth book, is in many ways his most personal. In it he considers his unique life of faith and belief in God. Autry is a former Fortune 500 executive, author, poet, and consultant whose work has had a significant influence on leadership thinking.

978-157312-484-3 144 pages/pb ***$16.00***

Making the Timeless Word Timely

A Primer for Preachers

Michael B. Brown

Michael Brown writes, "There is a simple formula for sermon preparation that creates messages that apply and engage whether your parish is rural or urban, young or old, rich or poor, five thousand members or fifty." The other part of the task, of course, involves being creative and insightful enough to know how to take the general formula for sermon preparation and make it particular in its impact on a specific congregation. Brown guides the reader through the formula and the skills to employ it with excellence and integrity.

978-1-57312-578-9 160 pages/pb ***$16.00***

Meeting Jesus Today

For the Cautious, the Curious, and the Committed

Jeanie Miley

Meeting Jesus Today, ideal for both individual study and small groups, is intended to be used as a workbook. It is designed to move readers from studying the Scriptures and ideas within the chapters to recording their journey with the Living Christ.

978-1-57312-677-9 320 pages/pb ***$19.00***

The Ministry Life

101 Tips for New Ministers

John Killinger

Sharing years of wisdom from more than fifty years in ministry and teaching, *The Ministry Life: 101 Tips for New Ministers* by John Killinger is filled with practical advice and wisdom for a minister's day-to-day tasks as well as advice on intellectual and spiritual habits to keep ministers of any age healthy and fulfilled. *978-1-57312-662-5 244 pages/pb* ***$19.00***

Mount and Mountain

Vol. 1: A Reverend and a Rabbi Talk About the Ten Commandments

Rami Shapiro and Michael Smith

Mount and Mountain represents the first half of an interfaith dialogue—a dialogue that neither preaches nor placates but challenges its participants to work both singly and together in the task of reinterpreting sacred texts. Mike and Rami discuss the nature of divinity, the power of faith, the beauty of myth and story, the necessity of doubt, the achievements, failings, and future of religion, and, above all, the struggle to live ethically and in harmony with the way of God. *978-1-57312-612-0 144 pages/pb* ***$15.00***

Mount and Mountain

Vol. 2: A Reverend and a Rabbi Talk About the Sermon on the Mount

Rami Shapiro and Michael Smith

This book, focused on the Sermon on the Mount, represents the second half of Mike and Rami's dialogue. In it, Mike and Rami explore the text of Jesus' sermon cooperatively, contributing perspectives drawn from their lives and religious traditions and seeking moments of illumination. *978-1-57312-654-0 254 pages/pb* ***$19.00***

Overcoming Adolescence

Growing Beyond Childhood into Maturity

Marion D. Aldridge

In *Overcoming Adolescence*, Marion D. Aldridge poses questions for adults of all ages to consider. His challenge to readers is one he has personally worked to confront: to grow up *all the way*—mentally, physically, academically, socially, emotionally, and spiritually. The key involves not only knowing how to work through the process but also how to recognize what may be contributing to our perpetual adolescence.

978-1-57312-577-2 156 pages/pb ***$17.00***

To order call 1-800-747-3016 or visit www.helwys.com

Psychic Pancakes & Communion Pizza

More Musings and Mutterings of a Church Misfit

Bert Montgomery

Psychic Pancakes & Communion Pizza is Bert Montgomery's highly anticipated follow-up to *Elvis, Willie, Jesus & Me* and contains further reflections on music, film, culture, life, and finding Jesus in the midst of it all. *978-1-57312-578-9 160 pages/pb* ***$16.00***

Quiet Faith

An Introvert's Guide to Spiritual Survival

Judson Edwards

In eight finely crafted chapters, Edwards looks at key issues like evangelism, interpreting the Bible, dealing with doubt, and surviving the church from the perspective of a confirmed, but sometimes reluctant, introvert. In the process, he offers some provocative insights that introverts will find helpful and reassuring. *978-1-57312-681-6 144 pages/pb* ***$15.00***

Reading Ezekiel (Reading the Old Testament series)

A Literary and Theological Commentary

Marvin A. Sweeney

The book of Ezekiel points to the return of YHWH to the holy temple at the center of a reconstituted Israel and creation at large. As such, the book of Ezekiel portrays the purging of Jerusalem, the Temple, and the people, to reconstitute them as part of a new creation at the conclusion of the book. With Jerusalem, the Temple, and the people so purged, YHWH stands once again in the holy center of the created world.

978-1-57312-658-8 264 pages/pb ***$22.00***

Reading Hosea–Micah (Reading the Old Testament series)

A Literary and Theological Commentary

Terence E. Fretheim

Terence E. Fretheim explores themes of indictment, judgment, and salvation in Hosea–Micah. The indictment against the people of God especially involves issues of idolatry, as well as abuse of the poor and needy. The effects of such behaviors are often horrendous in their severity. While God is often the subject of such judgments, the consequences, like fruit, grow out of the deed itself. *978-1-57312-687-8 224 pages/pb* ***$22.00***

To order call 1-800-747-3016 or visit www.helwys.com

Reading Samuel (Reading the Old Testament series)

A Literary and Theological Commentary

Johanna W. H. van Wijk-Bos

Interpreted masterfully by preeminent Old Testament scholar Johanna W. H. van Wijk-Bos, the story of Samuel touches on a vast array of subjects that make up the rich fabric of human life. The reader gains an inside look at leadership, royal intrigue, military campaigns, occult practices, and the significance of religious objects of veneration.

978-1-57312-607-6 272 pages/pb ***$22.00***

Sessions with Genesis (Session Bible Studies series)

The Story Begins

Tony W. Cartledge

Immersing us in the book of Genesis, Tony W. Cartledge examines both its major stories and the smaller cycles of hope and failure, of promise and judgment. Genesis introduces these themes of divine faithfulness and human failure in unmistakable terms, tracing Israel's beginning to the creation of the world and professing a belief that Israel's particular history had universal significance.

978-1-57312-636-6 144 pages/pb ***$14.00***

Sessions with Revelation (Session Bible Studies series)

The Final Days of Evil

David Sapp

David Sapp's careful guide through Revelation demonstrates that it is a letter of hope for believers; it is less about the last days of history than it is about the last days of evil. Without eliminating its mystery, Sapp unlocks Revelation's central truths so that its relevance becomes clear.

978-1-57312-706-6 166 pages/pb ***$14.00***

Silver Linings

My Life Before and After *Challenger 7*

June Scobee Rodgers

We know the public story of *Challenger 7*'s tragic destruction. That day, June's life took a new direction that ultimately led to the creation of the Challenger Center and to new life and new love. Her story of Christian faith and triumph over adversity will inspire readers of every age.

978-1-57312-570-3 352 pages/hc ***$28.00***

978-1-57312-694-6 352 pages/pb ***$18.00***

To order call 1-800-747-3016 or visit www.helwys.com

Spacious

Exploring Faith and Place

Holly Sprink

Exploring where we are and why that matters to God is an ongoing process. If we are present and attentive, God creatively and continuously widens our view of the world. *978-1-57312-649-6 156 pages/pb* **$16.00**

The Teaching Church

Congregation as Mentor

Christopher M. Hamlin / Sarah Jackson Shelton

Collected in *The Teaching Church: Congregation as Mentor* are the stories of the pastors who shared how congregations have shaped, nurtured, and, sometimes, broken their resolve to be faithful servants of God. *978-1-57312-682-3 112 pages/pb* **$13.00**

A Time to Laugh

Humor in the Bible

Mark E. Biddle

An extension of his well-loved seminary course on humor in the Bible, *A Time to Laugh* draws on Mark E. Biddle's command of Hebrew language and cultural subtleties to explore the ways humor was intentionally incorporated into Scripture. With characteristic liveliness, Biddle guides the reader through the stories of six biblical characters who did rather unexpected things. *978-1-57312-683-0 164 pages/pb* **$14.00**

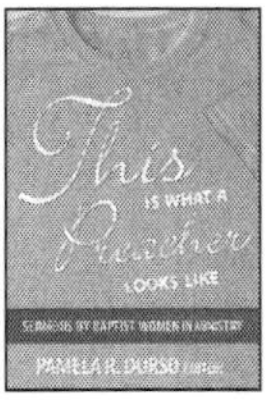

This Is What a Preacher Looks Like

Sermons by Baptist Women in Ministry

Pamela Durso, ed.

In this collection of sermons by thirty-six Baptist women, their voices are soft and loud, prophetic and pastoral, humorous and sincere. They are African American, Asian, Latina, and Caucasian. They are sisters, wives, mothers, grandmothers, aunts, and friends.

978-1-57312-554-3 144 pages/pb **$18.00**

William J. Reynolds

Church Musician

David W. Music

William J. Reynolds is renowned among Baptist musicians, music ministers, song leaders, and hymnody students. In eminently readable style, David W. Music's comprehensive biography describes Reynolds's family and educational background, his career as a minister of music, denominational leader, and seminary professor. *978-1-57312-690-8 358 pages/pb* **$23.00**

To order call 1-800-747-3016 or visit www.helwys.com

6542253R00077

Printed in Great Britain
by Amazon.co.uk, Ltd.,
Marston Gate.